ANGLES
ON THE ENGLISH-SPEAKING WORLD

VOLUME 4

*Writing and Vocabulary
in Foreign Language Acquisition*

Editors: Dorte Albrechtsen,
Kirsten Haastrup and Birgit Henriksen

ANGLES ON THE ENGLISH-SPEAKING WORLD

VOLUME 4

*Writing and Vocabulary
in Foreign Language Acquisition*

Editors: Dorte Albrechtsen,
Kirsten Haastrup and Birgit Henriksen

Published for
The Department of English,
University of Copenhagen

*

EDITORIAL BOARD

DORTE ALBRECHTSEN RUSSELL DUNCAN

LENE ØSTERMARK-JOHANSEN

BOOK REVIEW EDITOR
CHARLES LOCK

*

Angles on the English-Speaking World is published once a year by the Department of English at the University of Copenhagen. Issues are thematic and contain a balance of articles from local and international contributors. *Angles* is intended as a lively forum for a broad range of literary, linguistic, cultural and historical studies from various theoretical standpoints.

*

Articles for consideration and all editorial communication should be sent in three copies to:
Angles on the English-Speaking World
University of Copenhagen, Department of English
Njalsgade 130, DK-2300 Copenhagen S, Denmark

Business communications, including subscriptions and orders for reprints, should be addressed to the publishers:

MUSEUM TUSCULANUM PRESS
Njalsgade 94, DK-2300 Copenhagen S, Denmark
www.mtp.dk

*

Cover design by Henrik Maribo based on a hand-coloured engraving entitled *Monde dans une tête de fou* (ca. 1590). Bibliothèque nationale de France.

Set by Sanne Larsen and Anna Henneberg

Printed in Denmark by KOPI SERVICE at the Faculty of Humanities, University of Copenhagen

© 2004 MUSEUM TUSCULANUM PRESS &
ANGLES ON THE ENGLISH-SPEAKING WORLD
New Series, volume 4

ISBN 87-7289-932-8
ISSN 0903-1723

CONTENTS

Editors' Preface 7

Luxin Yang, Kyoko Baba, and Alister Cumming
Activity Systems for ESL Writing Improvement:
Case Studies of Three Chinese and Three Japanese
Adult Learners of English 13

Alister Cumming, Keanre Eouanzoui,
Guillaume Gentil, and Luxin Yang
Scaling Changes in Learners' Goals for
Writing Improvement over an ESL Course............................ 35

Dorte Albrechtsen, Kirsten Haastrup, and Birgit Henriksen
Attention to Argumentation in Learner Text Production:
How do We Capture Learner Ability in Argumentation?.................. 51

Anna Cieślicka and David Singleton
Metaphorical Competence and the L2 Learner 69

Paul Meara and Brent Wolter
V_Links: Beyond Vocabulary Depth.. 85

Rob Waring and Paul Nation
Second Language Reading and Incidental Vocabulary Learning 97

Kirsten Haastrup, Dorte Albrechtsen, and Birgit Henriksen
Lexical Inferencing Processes in L1 and L2:
Same or Different? Focus on Issues in Design and Method 111

Birgit Henriksen, Dorte Albrechtsen, and Kirsten Haastrup
The Relationship between Vocabulary Size and
Reading Comprehension in the L2 129

Review Article

Ulf Hedetoft
The Scholarship of Paranationalism
A review of Jørgen Sevaldsen, editor, *Britain and Denmark:
Political, Economic and Cultural Relations
in the 19th and 20th Centuries* 141

Notes on Contributors 149

Forthcoming Issues 153

EDITORS' PREFACE

Introduction

This volume features eight articles on writing and vocabulary acquisition – two crucial areas of study in foreign language learning and teaching. Five contributions have come from notable research environments in Canada, Ireland, New Zealand, Poland and Wales, and we are most grateful that these authors have accepted our invitation to write an article for this issue of *Angles*.

Three articles derive from a collaborative project between researchers from the English departments of the University of Copenhagen and the Copenhagen Business School. This project was launched in 2001 when the editors of this volume received a large grant from the Danish Research Council for the Humanities for the furtherance of a research programme under the title: *Processes in writing and vocabulary acquisition in English as a foreign language*.[1]

That generous award has provided us with the financial means to strengthen already existing links with scholars in other countries, and to establish new contacts. Among the initiatives taken as a result were invitations to experts in the field to come to Denmark to give guest lectures. In addition, the funding enabled us to recruit researchers from other countries as consultants for the project and visits were made by us to colleagues in other countries, which provided us with stimulation and many new ideas.

We want at this point to specify the research centres, and the individual scholars, from whose expertise we have benefited in so many ways. Colleagues from these institutions have provided us with inspiration for our project, and several have contributed papers to this volume.

A link with the Ontario Institute of Studies in Education (OISE), Canada, was established in the 1970s between the late Claus Færch (University of Copenhagen) and Merrill Swain (Modern Language Centre at OISE, University of Toronto). The contact with OISE has been kept up over the years and further strengthened through our present co-operation with Alister Cumming (Head of the Modern Language Centre) and Razika Sanaoui (York University, Toronto).

We are fortunate that our international network also includes three distinguished centres for vocabulary acquisition research: 'The Vocabulary Acquisition Research Group' at the University of Wales, Swansea, represented here by an article from Paul Meara and Brent Wolter; The School of Linguistics and Applied Language Studies at Victoria University, Wellington, New Zealand, represented by an article from Robert Waring and Paul Nation; 'The Trinity College Dublin Modern Languages Research Project', Ireland, represented by an article written by David Singleton (of Trinity) in co-operation with Anna Cieślicka from the Adam Mickiewicz University of Poznan, Poland.

Research on learner writing

The first section of this volume is devoted to studies of writing in a second or a foreign language (L2). The contributions address methodological issues for studying learner development in L2 writing. The research team from the Ontario Institute for Studies in Education have contributed two articles to this volume. In these, they report on investigations of student goals with respect to acquiring the writing skills needed to be able to cope in the discourse community of North American universities. Their data derive from interviews with 45 students at the beginning and at the end of a composition course. The analyses reported in this volume are from the first year of a longitudinal study.

In *Activity Systems for ESL Writing Improvement: Case Studies of three Chinese and three Japanese Adult Learners of English*, Yang, Baba and Cumming investigate the goals of six students, using activity theory to examine the possible changes in students' goals over one semester of composition instruction. This theoretical framework gives scope for an investigation of how external factors, such as the learning environment, assistance from other people, and the use of sources of various kinds, all interact with internal factors, such as motivation, beliefs and goals. Their mode of presentation allows ample space for the voices of the individual students to be heard. In the context of this volume, it is worth noting that a major goal for the students was improvement of their vocabulary.

In the second article, *Scaling Changes in Learners' Goals for Writing Improvement over an ESL Course*, Cumming, Eouanzoui, Gentil and Yang analyse the goals of all 45 of the students mentioned above. They apply an innovative method of analysis, termed dual-scaling, that can handle categorical data and enables the research team to capture not only the many factors involved in developing writing skills, but also the variability of this development in a group of learners from many different language backgrounds. The dual-scaling method produces plotted graphs of the students' responses which reveal either clustering of responses in relation to the goal variables investigated, or lack of such clustering, thereby providing a firm basis for the interpretation of the students' responses.

The last article in this section reports on work within the above-mentioned project *Processes in writing and vocabulary acquisition in English as a foreign language*. The aim of the project with respect to writing is to trace the development of writing skills in learners at three educational levels, namely Grade 7, Grade 10 and first year university. The focus in the investigation is on argumentative text production in both L2 and L1. In the article entitled ***Attention to Argumentation in Learner Text Production: How do We Capture Learner Ability in Argumentation?***, Albrechtsen, Haastrup and Henriksen address the issue of the limitations of verbal protocols. The article investigates the assumption that verbal reports produced by learners while engaged on a restricted writing task can supply information on learners' ability to argue in writing-information that might not be captured in verbal protocols produced while composing essays.

Vocabulary acquisition

Vocabulary was once regarded as a peripheral area of second language acquisition, as compared with the central position held by grammar, but lexical research has for a long time now been established as a flourishing field of study in its own right. The five contributions on vocabulary acquisition in this volume illustrate the wide scope and great breadth of the issues open to investigation, each paper offering a different perspective on vocabulary acquisition.

Singleton and Cieślicka, in their article ***Metaphorical Competence and the L2 learner,*** have philosophy of language and cognitive linguistics as their major sources of inspiration. Since Lakoff and Johnson's (1980) classic *Metaphors we Live By*, the view of metaphor in language studies has undergone a change, and in this paper the authors concentrate on the conceptual metaphor view of figurative language. Their discussion is reinforced by insights from cross-linguistic influences and bilingual processing; however, as the title suggests, they go much further, proceeding to discuss recent research on the acquisition of metaphorical competence in a foreign language, including Cieślicka's findings from a project on Polish learners' processing of English figurative language. In addition, the authors explain how theoretical findings may be applied to foreign language teaching.

A second perspective on vocabulary acquisition is provided by Meara and Wolter's contribution ***V-Links: Beyond Vocabulary Depth***. To characterise the nature of the vocabulary research initiated by Meara and his colleagues – a group one may refer to as the 'Swansea school' – one needs to invoke such key concepts as psycholinguistics, organisation of the mental lexicon, and experimental methods. Along with Meara's firm belief in the need for using formal models in vocabulary acquisition research, there is also an applied strand running clearly through the work of the Swansea school, namely the development of instruments for language testing. In their contribution to this volume, the authors take up certain issues much debated in the field of vocabulary research: What exactly needs to be included in the construct of vocabulary knowledge? What role is played by the size of the individual's vocabulary? (How many words does he or she know?) In what ways are words stored in the learner's mental lexicon? (How is a particular word linked to other words?) Meara and Wolter argue that both size and organisation are significant dimensions of lexical competence and elaborate on the latter aspect through presenting recent work on the development of a new test for measuring the organisational structure of the lexicon.

The title of Waring and Nation's paper, *Second Language Reading and Incidental Vocabulary Learning,* highlights the fact that they take up a third perspective – with reading research as a starting point. For a long time, language teachers have commonly held the notion that students will pick up new words in a foreign language through reading, especially if the content of the reading material appeals to them. Over the last decade or so, the validity of this belief has been investigated under the heading of 'incidental vocabulary learning'. Waring and Nation review empirical studies that have attempted to measure the actual effect of reading on vocabulary acquisition. They endeavour to answer the question of just how many words students actually do acquire through reading, taking into account that typically the learners will be concentrating on meaning of the content as a whole, rather than linguistic matters such as individual words. A further research motivation behind the article is the authors' interest in vocabulary teaching issues – not least in language teaching materials such as graded readers.

The last two articles in the vocabulary section report on work from the Danish research project mentioned at the outset. The aim of that project with respect to vocabulary acquisition is to investigate the structure of the learner lexicon and lexical inferencing processes in both L1 and L2 across the three educational levels previously mentioned. (Note that the sub-study on network organisation, which directly links to issues raised in Meara and Wolter's article, is not dealt with in this volume; for a preliminary presentation of this work, see Albrechtsen, Haastrup and Henriksen, 2003.) The sub-study on lexical inferencing, reported on by Haastrup, Albrechtsen and Henriksen in this volume, reflects issues discussed in Waring and Nation's paper. A major source of inspiration for the study of lexical inferencing is comprehension research and text inferencing, notably in the context of L2 reading. The focus on unknown words and word guessing processes, however, highlights the vocabulary aspect, and thus places this investigation at a point in between studies in comprehension vis-à-vis those in vocabulary acquisition. The article by Henriksen, Albrechtsen and Haastrup also deals with the vocabulary and reading relationship, but in this case a test perspective is taken.

As mentioned above, Waring and Nation concentrate on how learners acquire words incidentally while reading. Haastrup, Albrechtsen and Henriksen's article *Lexical Inferencing Processes in L1 and L2 – Same or Different: Focus on Issues in Design and Method,* examines more closely the types of guessing processes involved when learners come across unknown vocabulary items in reading material, comparing the strategies of two learners both in their L1 (Danish), and their L2 (English). Cross-linguistic comparisons involving learners who differ markedly in terms of educational level need to be undertaken with great care, and require researchers to devise tasks which are as closely parallel as possible with regard to the selection of texts, the topics covered and the test words chosen. The article addresses these design issues and illustrates the type of protocol analysis involved in dealing with 'think-aloud' data.

The two previously mentioned contributions emphasise the fact that there is a strong relationship between vocabulary and reading. Most vocabulary acquisition appears to take place incidentally through reading, and a substantial knowledge and understanding of the vocabulary included in written texts are needed in order to be able to read well. Henriksen, Albrechtsen and Haastrup, in their article *The Relationship Between Vocabulary Size and Reading Comprehension in the L2,* explore this relationship, basing their analysis on selected testing data from the Danish elicitation battery.

Notes

[1] The editors welcome this chance to acknowledge their gratitude to the Danish National Research Council for the Humanities (Statens Humanistiske Forskningsråd) for the three-year research grant which has made this project possible. We thank the participating informants as well as the many students who have assisted us with respect to data collection and many hours of data transcription. We wish to express out sincere gratitude to our research assistant Sanne Larsen not only for her great talent for organisation but notably for her insightful ideas and comments on our research. Without her dedication, the project would not have been possible.

References

Albrechtsen, D., Haastrup K. and Henriksen, B. (2003) 'Processes in Foreign Language Writing and Vocabulary Acquisition: Learner Development in L1 and L2', in Haastrup, K. (ed.) *Studies in Second Language Acquisition: Focus on Writing and Vocabulary Development in a Foreign Language.* Copenhagen Working Papers in LSP, **7**, 16-70.

ACTIVITY SYSTEMS FOR ESL WRITING IMPROVEMENT: CASE STUDIES OF THREE CHINESE AND THREE JAPANESE ADULT LEARNERS OF ENGLISH

Luxin Yang, Kyoko Baba, and Alister Cumming

ABSTRACT

We interviewed 3 Chinese and 3 Japanese learners about their goals for improving their writing in English near the beginning and the end of a pre-university ESL program. The students expressed goals and actions related to: the rhetoric of their first and second languages, their vocabulary and grammar, support from their teachers, and diverse individual actions. Using activity theory to interpret changes between the first and second interviews, we observe that these students maintained the basic rules and division of labor in their ESL classes but modified slightly their uses of mediating artifacts and community to achieve learning outcomes.

Introduction

An increasing population of students of English as a Second Language (ESL) has, over the past two decades, been pursuing higher education in North American universities. In turn, a growing body of research has investigated how these ESL students write in English-dominant universities (Cumming 2001). Most of these studies have described ESL students' writing performance through analyses of their written products and/or composing processes. Recently, attention has shifted to understanding how ESL students actually learn to write. For instance, several longitudinal studies have examined, in illuminating ways, the development of ESL students' writing abilities within particular academic settings. Some studies have focused on undergraduate students (e.g. Currie 1993; Johns 1992; Leki 1995, 1999; Spack 1997) and others on graduate students (e.g. Angelova and Riazantseva 1999; Casanave 1992; Riazi 1997; Silva 1992). Few studies, however, have attempted to explain how ESL students learn to write in academic English prior to university studies (Basturkmen and Lewis 2002; Cumming and Riazi 2000). In the present article we take up this challenge, using activity theory as a theoretical framework to explain how six ESL students were learning to improve their writing in a semester-long, intensive, pre-university ESL program at a major Canadian university[1].

Activity Theory

The principles of activity theory were initiated by Vygotsky (1978) and further developed by Leont'ev (1978, 1981) and Engeström (1987, 1999). Essentially, activity theory holds that human beings construct their knowledge through their interactions with others and the world. This framework provides an important foundation for research into the roles played by teachers, students, and social contexts in learning interactions (e.g. Lee 2000; Wertsch 1985). As Ares and Peercy (2003: 634) argued, 'This perspective enlarges our understanding of learning to acknowledge that students reproduce and transform culturally, socially grounded knowledge and skills, and appropriate various roles that are part of participation in social groups.' Such notions of learning assert that individual students are active, responsible agents with their own individual goals, orientations, values, beliefs, and histories, and each person constructs learning activities in unique ways (Cole 1996; Donato 2000; Lantolf and Pavlenko 1995). That is, learners choose what is salient to them and take actions toward their goals. They 'do not simply internalize and appropriate the consequences of activities on the social plane,' but also 'actively restructure their knowledge both with each other and within themselves' (John-Steiner and Meehan, 2001: 35). These internal tensions and contradictions contribute to the change and development of learning activity (Engeström and Miettinen 1999). The properties of any activity are determined by its socio-historical setting, mediational means, and participants' goals and socio-cultural histories (Leont'ev 1981). Thus, to understand learning processes, we need to understand how individual learners engage with specific tasks, what they bring to such tasks, and how they act to fulfill the objectives they perceive for such tasks.

This theoretical framework shifts our focus of analysis from decontextualized variables (e.g. as in pre-constructed experimental tasks) to analyses of activity systems composed of individuals in their naturally occurring social contexts. Leont'ev (1978, 1981) proposed a scheme for analyzing an activity system in terms of ***activity, action,*** and ***operation*** and corresponding ***motive, goal,*** and ***instrument conditions.*** *Activities* are distinguished by their energizing *motives* (be they material or ideal), which are oriented by *objects*. *Actions* are goal-oriented processes of translating activities into reality. *Operations* are the results of the transformation of actions, depending directly on the situated conditions of actions. One activity may be undertaken with different actions; one and the same action can result in different activities. Likewise, similar actions may have different motives, whereas different actions may have similar motives. However, Leont'ev's activity model does not fully explicate the societal (or collective) and collaborative nature of an individual's actions. It does not address the multivoiced and multilayered nature of activities as a source of compartmentalization, conflict and contradiction that drive changes and transformation both within local activity systems and the psychology of their participants (Engeström 1999).

Engeström (1987, 1991, 1993) expanded Leont'ev's concept of activity by introducing the institutional dimension in terms of *rules, communities* and *division of labor*. Thus, an activity system contains *subject, object, mediating artifacts* (e.g. signs and tools), *rules, community* and *division of labor* (Cole and Engeström 1993). To take an example of second language (L2) learning, a student (*subject*) in an ESL class aims to improve her competence in academic English writing (*object*). This student may follow the teacher's instruction, do assignments, read a textbook, talk with friends, surf the Internet, refer to dictionaries and so on (*mediating artifacts*). After a period of practice this student may achieve her goal such as getting a high grade on her essays (*outcome*). This activity happens in the ESL class (*community*), and the student intends to grasp the conventions of academic English writing (*rules*). In this ESL class, the teacher provides model instruction, gives assignments, and offers feedback, and students follow their teacher and do the assignments (*division of labor*). Therefore, the activity of learning to write involves six multifaceted factors categorized as the **subject, object, mediating artifacts, rules, community** and **division of labor**. From this view, learning to write is not simply learning the textual conventions of a target language, but also learning to do the conventional acts of a particular community and thus becoming a functioning member of that community.

Writing Development in University Contexts

Principles of activity theory or related concepts—such as genre theory, social cognition, or semiotics—have featured in much of the recent research documenting the contextual factors and interactions that shape adults' development of writing abilities in academic settings. Studies of English mother-tongue composition (Berkenkotter, Huckin and Ackerman 1988, 1991; Chiseri-Strater 1991; Faigley and Hansen 1985; Herrington 1985, 1992; McCarthy 1987; Sternglass 1997; Walvoord and McCarthy 1990) show that native-English-speaking (NES) students face, at the beginning of their academic studies, fundamental challenges of transition to new, academic forms of literacy, learning as they interact with, and act on, the contexts they encounter to 'master the ways of speaking, reading and writing that are appropriate to the new community' (Berkenkotter et al. 1988: 12). Each course or instructor introduces subject matter and ways of interacting and writing that are, to some extent, new. Some students learn the ropes quickly, such as Dave in McCarthy (1987), whereas others progress slowly, such as Nick and Anna in Chiseri-Strater (1991).

The fluidity and variation in university writing produces particular challenges for ESL students who are, uniquely and by definition, linguistically and culturally distant from the English language and its associated institutional norms. Researchers have examined how various ESL university students have learned to cope with writing for their subject-related courses (e.g. Angelova and Riazantseva 1999; Casanave 1992; Currie 1993, 1998; Dong 1996; Fishman and McCarthy 2001; Johns 1992; Leki 1995, 1999, 2001, 2003; Prior 1998; Riazi 1997; Schneider and Fujishima 1995; Spack 1997), reconfigured their perceptions of academic writing in English (e.g. Hilgers et al. 1999; Leki and Carson 1997; Silva 1992), or set goals to improve their writing abilities (e.g. Cumming 1986; Cumming, Busch and Zhou 2002; Hoffman 1998). These studies collectively convey the image that ESL students actively construct their learning conditions by developing particular coping strategies to meet the demands of academic writing in English-medium universities. Moreover, acquiring L2 academic literacy is normally a lengthy, painstaking process of acquiring familiarity with the writing conventions of the university culture and its disciplinary subcultures but varying with students' 'linguistic and cognitive development, previous educational experiences, and cultural background as well as interactions with instructors and course-related texts' (Spack 1997: 6).

The Present Study

Following these principles, the present analyses show how activity theory can explain pre-university ESL students' development of context-specific writing skills. We selected for analyses the cases of three Chinese and three Japanese students who had participated in a larger study (involving 45 ESL students and 5 of their instructors) over a semester of an intensive pre-university ESL program. The overall research study was conceived to describe and trace the development of the goals for writing improvement that ESL learners and their instructors have (Cumming 2003; Cumming, Busch and Zhou 2002, see also the article by Cumming, Eounzaoui, Gentil and Yang, this volume). In the present analyses we addressed two research questions:

1) What goals did these students have for improving their writing in English in the context of an intensive, pre-university ESL program?
2) What actions did these ESL students take to achieve their writing goals in this context?

Method

Participants

All six participants were female and had volunteered for the research from an ESL academic preparation program at a major Canadian university. The three Chinese students (who we have called Yingxue, Xin, and Wenzhen) were from Mainland China and around 19 years old. The three Japanese students (who we have called Hana, Kazuko, and Rihoko) were in their early or mid 20s. Xin, Yingxue, Hana, Kazuko, and Rihoko all studied in an advanced-level ESL course, though Rihoko was in a different class from the other four students. Wenzhen studied in a high-intermediate-level ESL course. The students had all completed secondary school education in their native countries, where they had studied English as a foreign language for six to eight years. Kazuko had just started university studies in Japan before she came to Canada. The Chinese students had been studying in Canada for about nine months prior to the first interview, whereas Kazuko, Hana, and Rihoko had been studying for one year, six months, and one and a half years respectively. Yingxue planned to study for a master's degree in accounting; Xin, a doctoral degree in computer science or medicine; Wenzhen, a bachelor's degree in commerce or architecture; Kazuko, a doctoral degree in political science or psychology; and Rihoko, a bachelor's degree in biology. Hana was uncertain of her future studies, but she thought of studying cinematography. They all participated in this academic preparation program voluntarily to improve their English language proficiency prior to future university studies in Canada. We selected the three Chinese students for the present analysis because they had made (in comparison to the 11 other Chinese students participating in our study) notable progress in their English studies; Luxin Yang had interviewed each using both English and Mandarin. The three Japanese students were selected for comparison and because they comprised the full sample of Japanese students in our project; they had been interviewed in English (prior to Kyoko Baba's joining our project team), so data on their goals and activities appear less complete than those of the Chinese students.

Data collection and analysis

We collected from each student, near the beginning and the end of the ESL program, their responses to profile questionnaires, in-depth interviews of 30 to 90 minutes, and stimulated recalls of samples of their writing they had brought to the interviews. The interview schedule consisted of open-ended questions about the students' writing goals, writing practices, and difficulties in writing. The same interview questions were used for the two rounds of interviews and stimulated recalls in order to determine commonalities and differences between the beginning and end of the ESL course. Applying qualitative research methods of analytic induction (Goetz and LeCompte 1984) and constant comparison (Miles and Huberman 1994) to transcriptions of the interviews, we read the data carefully and repeatedly, searching for recurring themes or patterns related to the principles of activity theory, in addition to inspecting the students' written drafts to corroborate the participants' reflections and our interpretations of them.

Findings

Learning Intentions

The six students were all highly motivated and each worked hard to improve their English writing. Their long-term goals were to study in their fields of interest at a Canadian university. The Chinese students noted how they wished to fulfill the support of their parents, who had spent considerable sums of money to send them to study abroad. None of the six students had clear conceptualizations of what they might actually write in their future university studies, but they all expressed during the two interviews their intentions to learn to write as effectively as NES writers in terms of language use and content development. For example, Xin hoped that she could write in English as well as in her first language, Chinese, using English idioms or phrases freely. Kazuko, Hana and Rihoko, in particular, were concerned with improving their abilities for timed, in-class, essay exams or English proficiency tests.

L1/L2 Comparisons

The six students all remarked in their first interviews on differences in the conventions for writing between their L1 (Chinese or Japanese) and English, a point that had arisen from their ESL teachers' comments on their writing and their classroom instruction. Yingxue, Xin, and Wenzhen observed that English essay writing required a rigid 'three-step' format (i.e. introduction, body, and conclusion); whereas the organization of Chinese essays was more flexible. For instance, Wenzhen indicated that she paid little attention to rhetorical structure in her Chinese writing. She could get good marks on her Chinese writing so long as her language use was good. Wenzhen felt confused when her ESL teacher commented that she did not make her ideas clear in the first lengthy composition she did in the ESL course. Afterwards, to develop her arguments explicitly in English, Wenzhen took her friends' suggestions and started to follow a 'fixed' pattern for organizing her texts:

> Now when I came here, first time I wrote a longer writing [in English]. When I hand it in to [my] teacher, the teacher said, the sentence, your main idea is not clear. I'm confused, I don't know how to write this, but uh some of my friends also came here for longer time, … they suggest me, you just write like patterns, topic sentence, and reasons and conclusion, it's easy, just easy patterns, not use a lot of like describe, description, not like this, just write reason directly. Uh, now I change, I just follow this pattern.

Although they found the 'fixed pattern' somewhat boring, the three Chinese students all indicated that they would follow it in their English essay writing because it was expected by their teachers. Likewise, the three Japanese students stated that they were trying to follow English academic writing conventions by trying to make their claims or opinions clear with supporting details, and in particular, to use native-like sentence structures. Wenzhen, Kazuko and Hana also indicated that they felt they needed to state their arguments and positions at the beginning of their English essays and to make them clear, whereas in Chinese or Japanese, they could give their arguments in the middle or at the end or just imply what their arguments were. For example, Wenzhen commented,

> The pattern is different. The logic is different. In China, I learn to write…at the beginning of writing I didn't say something like…my opinion, not like this. You must read the whole composition, [then] you can know what my opinion [is] about this. Not the first sentence, so I think I should…change my logical [thinking] and opinion about this. I should adjust…like Canadian people, Canadians. Second, I think the Canadians like, people in North America, they like argument. But I'm not good at this, I think. Sometimes I have my opinion, but I don't like to give my opinions, like make a big speech, I don't, I just know my opinion. I'm not good at give my opinion to others. I should practice about this skill in the future in my writing, do more argument.

Similarly, Hana indicated that 'beautiful' language is an important criterion for Japanese writing, and supporting details are not necessary to make a claim or an argument:

> I heard that in this country's [Canada] essays I have to express my idea …at the very beginning of the essay and more directly, but in my culture…in my country [Japan], it is said that I have to use very beautiful word…

> I think so because I was in Japan I just do.. uh.. I just express my idea not like I didn't give any supporting details just what I was thinking, so, but in Canada I try to give some details which people say generally…so I think it's different.

The beauty of language tends to be highly valued in Chinese and Japanese writing (Li 1996; National Institute for Japanese Language 2002). Moreover, Chinese and Japanese readers seem accustomed to appreciating the use of ambiguous words with multiple connotations. As research on contrastive rhetoric has long argued, students educated to write in one society may have to modify the rhetorical schemata they have developed in that society when they come to write in other languages and contexts (Grabe and Kaplan 1996; Li 1996). However, it is also recognized that Chinese and Japanese rhetorical patterns could be plain, direct, and clear in one instance, and indirect, implicit, or paratactic in another instance (Kirkpatrick 1997; Kubota 1997). It is also worth observing that these six students had only completed secondary school education in their home countries, so they had not yet fully developed their L1 writing abilities, especially for academic writing.

Vocabulary
In order to achieve their goals, the six students recognized the importance of enlarging their English vocabularies. They could not express their ideas as fully and clearly in English as they did when writing in their first languages. So they felt frustrated repeating the same words or not being able to make their ideas understood in English: 'I always repeat my words again again again, so it's not like [an] essay' (Hana); 'When I cannot put my idea in English, I become frustrated' (Rihoko). They all said they tried to learn new words by reading more (particularly, newspapers, magazines, and books), watching TV, and practicing using new words in their writing. They also acknowledged that reading inspired them with ideas on a topic and helped them acquire such aspects of English writing style as native-like sentence structures, tone of expression, and organization of information. The students seemed overtly conscious of vocabulary learning in their writing, acknowledging that vocabulary is a key element in the evaluation of writing quality (e.g. Engber 1995; Grobe 1981) but also because vocabulary learning is a social act. Since word meanings are embedded in 'the background of assumptions, ideologies, values, beliefs and cultural experiences that comprise the meaning system' (Corson 1995: 51), people must become familiar with words and their meaning systems to communicate successfully. In this respect, Kazuko and Rihoko expressed desires

to learn words related to their future academic fields (i.e. political science, psychology, or biology), which was not the focus of their ESL instruction. For them, learning academic vocabulary meant not only writing effectively but also entering what Corson (1995) called an academic meaning system.

Grammar
All the participants intended to improve their grammatical performance in English writing. The three Chinese students specified minor grammar problems they experienced, such as the use of articles, prepositions and native-sounding sentence structures. The three Japanese students focused on varied types of clauses, tenses, and transitional words. Although the students had learned English grammar rules in high school, they still had difficulty applying their grammatical knowledge in writing. As Yingxue stated, 'I know all the [grammar] rules. But when I apply these grammar rules, I usually have problems with some grammar rules. It seems that articles are difficult for me. I'm not good at articles.' Or as Kazuko observed, 'I don't know how to reduce a sentence [make a sentence short]. What I mean is, like, my sentences are long and there is no proper sentence sometimes. So I want to know how to reduce the sentence, in order to make effective essay.' Yingxue likewise realized that she should avoid using certain Chinese rhetorical structures in her English writing: 'Sometimes, in Chinese, we can use interrogative sentences consecutively. But here, like [my teacher], she doesn't like this kind of sentences. I tried to write this kind of sentences in her class, and she didn't like it at all.' Both Yingxue and Hana observed that their thinking about ideas in their L1 first then translating them into English could result in awkward English expressions: 'Maybe that's why my essay sounds not smooth, because I try to translate, maybe this is a little bit different from, the expressions may be a little bit different from English, I mean the Chinese way.' (Yingxue); 'When I find it's too difficult to explain my ideas in English at first, I think about the topic in Japanese.' (Hana)

Teachers' Support
Their ESL instructors played important roles in the six students' learning experiences. The students all took their teachers' suggestions seriously, applying them diligently to their composing. For example, all the participants followed such suggestions for composing as brainstorming ideas and making an outline before they started to write. Kazuko, Hana and Rihoko admitted that they could not evaluate their English writing by themselves, and they hoped to learn relevant evaluation criteria from their teachers. They all appreciated what their teachers taught in classes and the usefulness of their

comments on their writing. As Xin stated:

> Uh, of course they give us assignments, after that they will point out the mistakes we've made and ask us to correct them by ourselves and later they will talk with us individually about our writing. Sometimes my teacher will give us a piece of writing, that kind of writing is just come from our classmates' journals, she asks us to correct it, correct this piece of writing and discuss it in our class. Uh, it is helpful, of course, it is helpful for that student. But I think the errors that she pointed out in this piece of writing must be representative, which will reflect our problems in our writings, so I feel it maybe, it is like we draw a lesson from other's mistakes. So I think it is very useful. And sometimes they will tell us some rules, grammar rules, she will give us, for example, when we learn about topic sentence, and supporting details, she will explain it to us, she give us a piece of paper with all the topic sentence, and ask us to write supporting details, this kind of thing. Uh, and what else? ... Always this kind of comment makes me pay attention to the problems, the teacher's questions, I will, of course, I will make some improvement, and ... anyway I learn from their comments...

Individual Actions for Learning Achievement

To achieve their learning goals, the six students told us about various actions they undertook to improve their writing. In their second interviews, they acknowledged distinct types of progress they had made in writing English. In the process, they appeared to shift the focus of their learning goals slightly. For example, Yingxue attempted to write essays more like NES writers by comparing or combining her ways of thinking in her L1 and L2. She could articulate the discrepancy between linguistic features in the English writing she did and those done by NES writers, for example, in respect to noun clauses:

> They [NES writers] will use some noun clauses or reduced clause to describe one thing, but if I write, maybe I will use some complex sentences such as uh adjective clause, but they can use reduced adjective clause, I can't actually, I don't know how to express things in a noun clause, on brief phrase, actually phrase, I just express them in a complex long clause.

Reading newspapers and novels were other ways that Yingxue said she learned about the organization of ideas in English texts. Instead of simply brainstorming her ideas on a paper, she asked herself questions on the topic first and then answered them. To make her English sound natural, she seldom used translation while composing. She continued using the three-step format in her essay writing, as she still did not know other formats. However, she paid special attention to sentence structures and word choices. She attempted to broaden her vocabulary with the aid of a Thesaurus. She also asked her ESL teacher to read and comment on her essays. Notably, outside of her ESL class, Yingxue approached her landlady's daughter (a senior high school student in Toronto) to ask her to comment on her drafts or for idiomatic expressions. For example, in describing one of her essays to us, Yingxue said, 'This is the comment from my landlord daughter, I just, I don't know how to express it well, … I told her in Chinese, and she gave me this sentence…' These efforts produced positive comments from Yingxue's teacher, 'A great response! Not because of what you say, but because how you say it! I congratulate you on a job well-done!' Yingxue was surprised and excited by her teacher's comments, increasing her confidence in her English writing: 'After I got A+ in [this composition], I feel a little bit better. I think if I ask someone to help me, to give me comments, and I do hard work on that, I can get a high mark on my writing, so am not so depressed.'

At the time of the second interview, Xin said that she felt she had already acquired the basic pattern of English essays, but she needed to improve her paragraph development. She aimed to make her arguments strong with sufficient and convincing details. To realize these goals, besides asking for her teacher's feedback, Xin started to borrow her classmate Yingxue's A or A+ papers, reading them carefully to see how Yingxue could get such high marks. Xin observed, 'I don't know how to write a response, something like this. I find that she [Yingxue] first focused on the topic well, and her structure was very well-organized, and she integrated her examples in her writing and she also used many new vocabularies and uh I feel that uh and her way of expressing her ideas is out of my expectation.' Xin also closely followed her teacher's instructions: 'Several days ago I just learned that, in the introduction, first step is background knowledge, second is restatement of the topic and third is the thesis statement. I know I don't need to, I don't have to follow this style, but maybe it's better because the teacher just taught us that thing, so I will do some, make some progress in the introduction, because introduction and conclusion are very important besides body paragraphs, uh it always give the readers first and last uh impression.' In her second interview, Xin brought a recent composition in which she received a B+ grade. Xin said she achieved 80% of her teacher's purposes, as shown in her teacher's comment, 'A much better essay, good example, clear and convincing. Introduction and conclusion are 100% better as are other supporting paragraphs.'

By the time of her second interview Wenzhen was confident about her organization of essays, but she admitted that she still had language problems. The essay she brought to the interview, according to her teacher, showed overall improvement in the aspects of content development, organization and language use, but she received a grade of B-. Her teacher commented, 'This paper showed good improvement from earlier drafts, with more focused and better-supported arguments. Things to concentrate on in the future are accuracy (grammar) and development of ideas. You need to consider all the possible angles of an issue and then decide which ones are most important to discuss in the space you have; don't begin by just identifying one or two things to talk about.' Likewise, word choice and expressing her ideas were still challenges for Wenzhen:

> Word choice, I think the meaning, if I translate it to my language, to Chinese, uh it's the same, it's correct, but when I use it, because the same meaning in Chinese will have several English words. The one you see it, I always choose the wrong word. … I think the word choice is my biggest problem.

> Something I think in my mind I know my position what I want to express, my ideas are very clear, but when I want to express on the paper, it becomes, sometimes confuse others. This is the problem.

To address these problems, Wenzhen started to memorize certain well-written paragraphs or sentences, recalling how she had learned English in high school in China, where her English teacher often asked the class to copy and memorize English texts. Wenzhen also decided to read more newspapers, magazines, and short essays. Wenzhen said she still depended on her teacher's feedback to identify her grammar errors.

The three Japanese students mainly worked with their classmates to discuss topics and exchange their compositions, and unlike Xin and Wenzhen they did not seek help outside their ESL class. Hana's classmates helped her with one essay by completing a survey questionnaire she used to gather information. Kazuko, Hana, and Rihoko followed their ESL teachers' suggestions closely. For example, in the second interview, Hana described how she tried to learn vocabulary in the ways suggested by her teacher, such as remembering a new word in a sentence and using it frequently. Similarly, Kazuko's teacher made her notice the importance of summarizing in academic writing by showing her a model essay from a second-year university student:

Uh, actually before my teacher gave me, the quite good writing ... from second year student at the university. And it was very good. And she, I thought I recognized that in the university I have to use a lot of, uh, a lot of opinion or writing from someone's book, or something, like that kind of thing. So, I thought, and she used something like special skill, to, to write someone's opinion. For example, 'the book says,' or 'according to the book,' that kind of thing. Anyway, she used a lot of information from someone's book, or writing, and in fact, anyway I think she summarized that kind of things in her way. So I think at the time I recognized it's important to summarize.

Subsequently, Kazuko started to practice summarizing source texts in her essay writing:

When I write essays, I have to, how to say, use sentence from books, or something like, from someone's writing. ... So, just I feel like that because I don't want to steal someone's writing, so I think I had better change the words, I had better summarize. ...Just I always do that, uh, I change someone's writing to my own style, ... just uh in my way, ... just I use my vocabulary that I know, and, maybe, make shorter.

Also, Kazuko broadened the focus of her goals from vocabulary and grammar to acquiring a native-like writing style: 'I am trying to use my own essay style and also academic style that I have to, for academic writing. And, actually it's so difficult, but I am trying to do that actually.' Instead of being nervous about English writing, Kazuko started to enjoy English writing. She also said she became more sensitive to word choices, trying to use difficult vocabulary and complex grammatical structures in her essay writing. However, this often resulted in awkward English in her teacher's eyes, to which Kazuko responded by trying to use concise, simple and effective phrases in her writing.

Hana appeared to gain, over the semester, strategic control over her composing processes. In her initial interview, Hana just described the content of her composition to us, paragraph by paragraph. In her second interview, Hana took a meta-perspective on her composition, explaining her goals for (rather than just the content of) each paragraph, showing how she attended to the essay's organization, especially the different roles that each paragraph performed: 'At first before I wrote this, we had time to write only just an introduction [in the class], and we developed the essay from that [after class]. At first I had a goal to make a great introduction. .... Before I wrote the essay my teacher gave me some advice only for the introduction... and I developed the paragraphs from it.' Hana displayed a conscious regard for the organization and fluency of her writing. In turn, she came to feel comfortable with English writing. Hana frequently asked her sister or parents for professional information on the topics she wrote about, though they did not explicitly help her to do her English writing.

Discussion: Changes in Activity Systems

We can understand the changes that these six students made in their learning goals in reference to Engeström's expanded notion of activity systems. Figure 1 follows Engeström's (1987) schema of an expanded activity system, indicating in respect to two triangles the potential changes that a hypothetical Student A could have made in learning goals in respect to the activity systems experienced at Interview 1 and then at Interview 2 in terms of objects, mediating artifacts, rules, communities, divisions of labor and outcomes. The position of Object 1 and Object 2 are opposite each other in each triangle merely to indicate that there was a single common outcome (i.e. change) between the two interviews. The six students in the present study did not change the rules or division of labor during the two interviews, so the relevant content of rules and division of labor are listed in Figure 1. However, each participant made certain changes in objects, mediating artifacts, communities, and outcomes, so we have listed the details of these changes in Table 1.

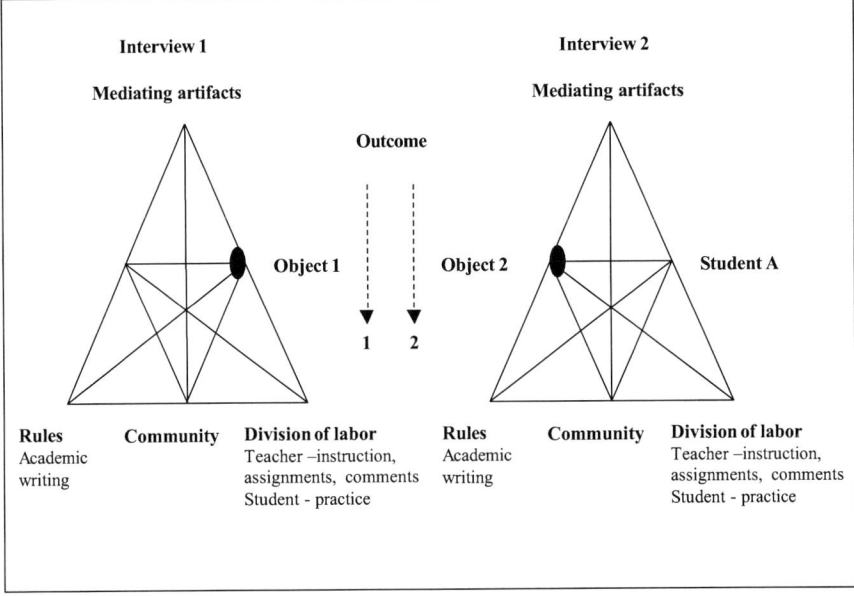

Figure 1. Activity systems in Interviews 1 and 2

Table 1. Comparison of Interviews 1 and 2

	Object	Mediating artifacts	Community	Outcome
Yingxue, Interview 1	Improving writing style in English	Teachers, free writing, newspaper, computer, dictionary	ESL Class	Depressed with her grade of C
Yingxue Interview 2	Thinking like NES writer	Teachers, NES writer, newspaper & novel, computer, planning, dictionary	ESL class; NES writer	Feel better with grades of (A/A+)
Xin Interview 1	Language improvement (e.g., vocabulary, sentence structure)	Teachers, newspaper & magazine, TV, dictionary, internet	ESL Class	Depressed with her incompetent ability to express herself in English
Xin Interview 2	Content development (e.g., supporting details), language (proper words)	Teachers, capable peer, newspaper & magazine, planning, dictionary, internet	ESL class; capable peer	Feeling better with grade of B+
Wenzhen Interview 1	Essay writing (e.g., organization, grammar)	Teachers, newspaper & textbooks, dictionary	ESL Class	Depressed with her grade of C-
Wenzhen Interview 2	Content development (convincing examples), grammar (word choice)	Teachers, model essays, dictionary	ESL Class	Improvement with grade of B-
Hana Interview 1	Grammar, vocabulary, organization, arguments	Teachers, textbooks, dictionaries, newspaper, internet, classmatesê writings, sister & parents	ESL class	Having difficulty writing clearly, e.g., in free writing
Hana Interview 2	Research skills, vocabulary, organization, write quickly	Teachers, books, newspaper, materials from her teacher, internet, classmatesêwritings, sister & parents, friends & neighbors	ESL class	Feeling more comfortable with grade of B-, metacognitive awareness of writing
Kazuko Interview 1	Grammar, formal vocabulary, concise sentences	Teachers, books, magazines, textbooks, dictionaries, grammar books, internet, classmatesê essays	ESL class	Better organization, feeling frustrated, nervous, & mental challenges
Kazuko Interview 2	Native-like sentence structure, academic vocabulary, writing style.	Teachers, dictionaries, well-written essays, internet, books, magazines, grammar books, classmatesêessays	ESL class	Loves to write, more sensitive to word choice, change in her view on academic writing, grade of B-
Rihoko Interview 1	Formal vocabulary, reduce grammar mistakes, sentence structure, fluent English	Teachers, newspaper, textbooks, dictionaries, outline.	ESL class	Sometimes frustrated but most of the time enjoys writing
Rihoko Interview 2	Grammar (esp. clauses), academic expressions	Teachers, newspaper, books, dictionaries, outlines.	ESL class	Sometimes frustrated

As shown in Figure 1 and Table 1, the *rules* and *division of labor* of their activity systems remained essentially the same for each participant (*subject*) over a semester of ESL studies. That is, the participants were still learning the conventions of academic writing in English. In this ESL program, teachers provided models of writing, gave assignments, and offered feedback on students' essays. Yingxue, Xin, Wenzhen, Hana, Kazuko, and Rihoko followed and practiced what their teachers taught by completing the prescribed assignments. Over the semester of ESL studies the *object* of Yingxue's goals remained essentially identical, but she shifted her writing goals from improving her writing style to thinking like a NES writer. Xin expanded her primary goal for her writing from language improvement to include content development as well. Wenzhen altered her writing goals from essay writing in general to content development (e.g. to provide convincing examples) and language use (e.g. word choice). Hana became more conscious of her essay organization and fluency in writing. Kazuko focused more on acquiring a NES writing style in addition to language improvement toward the end of the semester. Rihoko, however, did not change the objects of her writing goals in any obvious ways between her first and second interviews with us.

The students changed their *mediating artifacts, community*, and *outcomes* slightly between the two interviews. For *mediating artifacts*, besides continuously getting help from her teachers, and reading extensively, Wenzhen started to pay more attention to reading model essays to learn the development of content and appropriate expressions. Xin began to read newspapers or magazines, used dictionaries, surfed the Internet, and started to seek help from her peer, Yingxue, by reading her essays. Yingxue mentioned that she read English novels to learn how ideas were organized, she took a meta-perspective in her planning processes (i.e. by asking herself questions as a reader and then answering them instead of just brainstorming ideas into words), and sought comments from NES writers on her initial drafts prior to her teachers' feedback. Kazuko tried to read widely, especially well-written essays, and tried to strengthen her grammatical competence. All three Japanese students used various types of dictionaries as well as read textbooks, newspapers or magazines. All the participants relied greatly on their ESL teachers in their processes of learning to write academic English. Indeed, their ESL teachers were the central figure in each ESL student's community. Wenzhen, Xin and the three Japanese participants retained the same communities over the semester, that is, their ESL classes, including both their teachers and classmates. However, Hana actively searched information on her writing topics from her family in Japan and her friends or neighbours as well as surfing the Internet and reading books. Xin introduced the assistance of a *capable peer* into the broad community of her ESL class. By reading Yingxue's essays, Xin aimed to overcome her deficiency in content development and language use. Yingxue extended her *community* from her ESL class to a NES writer outside the class.

These slight changes in the students' *mediating artifacts* and *community* showed them to be active in their learning to write in English. In particular, the six students all adjusted their goals for writing improvement based on their perceptions of their writing problems. They introduced new mediating artifacts to achieve their writing goals when necessary and as prompted by their teachers' instructional activities (e.g. modeling writing, providing feedback, encouraging multiple drafts). As other researchers have observed with other ESL learners in other contexts, these students figured out their teachers' expectations and attempted to meet their requirements (e.g. Currie 1998; Johns 1992; Leki 1995; Spack 1997). These efforts brought positive *outcomes* at the end of the semester, although the degree of progress differed for each student. We think that activity theory explains these processes in reference to the contexts in which they occurred. These case studies testify that learning to write in a second language is both an internal process (e.g. involving goals, motivation, and beliefs) and the product of external factors (e.g. the learning environment, assistance from others, uses of mediating artifacts). However, we have to recognize that a single semester is a brief period to observe ESL writing development and that interviews reveal only partial aspects of these learning processes. For this reason we have followed these students for a further year as they entered university courses, and we are now, in another set of analyses, attempting to document how their goals and activity systems for improving their ESL writing changed in the context of studying in and writing for university courses in academic English.

Notes

[1] We gratefully acknowledge funding for this research through grant 410-2001-0791 from the Social Sciences and Humanities Research Council of Canada to Alister Cumming. We thank the participating students and teachers as well other members of the research team working on this project, who assisted in developing the research instruments and various aspects of data collection and analysis: Michael Busch, Jill Cummings, Keanre Eouanzoui, Usman Erdosy, Cheryl Fretz, Guillaume Gentil, Tae-Young Kim, and Ally Zhou.

References

Angelova, M. and Riazantseva, A. (1999) 'If You Don't Tell Me, How Can I Know? A Case Study of Four International Students Learning to Write the U.S. Way', *Written Communication*, **16**, 491-525.

Ares, N. and Peercy, M. (2003) 'Constructing Literacy: How Goals, Activity Systems, and Text Shape Classroom Practice', *Journal of Literacy Research*, **35**, 633-662.

Basturkmen, H. and Lewis, M. (2002) 'Learner Perspectives of Success in an EAP Writing Course', *Assessing Writing*, **8**, 31-46.

Berkenkotter, C., Huckin, T. and Ackerman, J. (1988) 'Conventions, Conversations, and the Writer: A Case Study of a Student in a Rhetoric Ph.D. Program', *Research in the Teaching of English*, **22**, 9-45.

Berkenkotter, C., Huckin, T. and Ackerman, J. (1991) 'Social Context and Socially Constructed Texts: The Initiation of a Graduate Student into a Writing Research Community', in C. Bazerman and J. Paradis (eds.), *Textual Dynamics of the Professions*, 191-215, University of Wisconsin Press: Madison, WI.

Casanave, C. (1992) 'Cultural Diversity and Socialization: A Case Study of a Hispanic Woman in a Doctoral Program in Sociology', in D. E. Murray (ed.), *Diversity as Resource: Redefining Cultural Literacy*, 148-182, Teachers of English to Speakers of Other Languages: Alexandria, VA.

Chiseri-Strater, E. (1991) *Academic Literacies: The Public and Private Discourse of University Students*, Boynton/Cook Publishers: Portsmouth, NH.

Cole, M. (1996) *Cultural Psychology: A Once and Future Discipline*, MA, Belknap Press: Cambridge.

Cole, M. and Engeström, Y. (1993) 'A cultural-historical approach to distributed cognition', in G. Salomon (ed.), *Distributed Cognitions: Psychological and Educational Considerations*, 1-46, Cambridge University Press: New York.

Corson, D. (1995) *Using English Words*, Kluwer Academic: Dordrecht, The Netherlands.

Cumming, A. (1986) 'Intentional Learning as a Principle for ESL Writing Instruction: A Case Study', in P. Lightbown and S. Firth (eds.), *TESL Canada Journal*, Special Issue **1**, 69–83.

Cumming, A. (2001) 'Learning to Write in a Second Language: Two Decades of Research,' in R. Manchon (ed.), *International Journal of English Studies*, Special Issue, *Writing in the L2 Classroom: Issues in Research and Pedagogy*, **1**, 2, 1-23.

Cumming, A. (2003) 'What are Students' Goals for Improving Their ESL Writing?', *TESL Ontario Contact*, **29**, 2, 34-37.

Cumming, A., Busch, M. and Zhou, A. (2002) 'Investigating Learners' Goals in the Context of Adult Second-language Writing', in G. Rijlaarsdam (Series ed.) and S. Ransdell and M. Barbier (Volume eds.), *Studies in Writing*, **11**: *New Directions for Research in L2 Writing*, 189-208, Kluwer Academic: Dordrecht, The Netherlands.

Cumming, A. and Riazi, A. (2000) 'Building Models of Adult Second-language Writing Instruction', *Learning and Instruction*, **10**, 55-71.

Currie, P. (1993) 'Entering a Disciplinary Community: Conceptual Activities Required to Write for One Introductory University Course', *Journal of Second Language Writing*, **2**, 101-117.

Currie, P. (1998) 'Staying Out of Trouble: Apparent Plagiarism and Academic Survival', *Journal of Second Language Writing*, **7**, 1-18.

Donato, R. (2000) 'Sociocultural Contributions to Understanding the Foreign and Second Language Classroom', in J. Lantolf (ed.), *Sociocultural Theory and Second Language Learning*, 27-50, Oxford University Press: Oxford.

Dong, Y. (1996) 'Learning How to Use Citations for Knowledge Transformation: Nonnative Doctoral Students' Dissertation Writing in Science', *Research in the Teaching of English*, **30**, 428-457.

Engber, C. (1995) 'The Relationship of Lexical Proficiency to the Quality of ESL Compositions', *Journal of Second Language Writing*, **4**, 2, 139-155.

Engeström, Y. (1987) *Learning by Expanding: An Activity-theoretical Approach to Developmental Research*, Orienta-Konsultit: Helsinki.

Engeström, Y. (1991) 'Activity Theory and Individual and Social Transformation', *Activity Theory*, **8** and **9**, 6-17.

Engeström, Y. (1993) 'Developmental Studies of Work as a Testbench of Activity Theory: The Case of Primary Care Medical Practice', in S. Chaiklin and J. Lave (eds.), *Understanding Practice: Perspectives on Activity and Context*, 64-103, Cambridge University Press: New York.

Engeström, Y. (1999) 'Activity Theory and Individual and Social Transformation', in Y. Engeström, R. Miettinen, and R. Punamaki (eds.), *Perspectives on Activity Theory*, 19-38, Cambridge University Press: Cambridge.

Engeström, Y. and Miettinen, R. (1999) 'Introduction', in Y. Engestrom, R. Miettinen, and R. Punamaki (eds.), *Perspectives on Activity Theory*, 1-16, Cambridge University Press: Cambridge.

Faigley, L. and Hansen, K. (1985) 'Learning to Write in the Social Sciences', *College Composition and Communication*, **36**, 140-149.

Goetz, J. P. and LeCompte, M.D. (1984) *Ethnography and Qualitative Design in Educational Research*, Academic Press: Orlando, FL.

Fishman, S. and McCarthy, L. (2001) 'An ESL Writer and Her Discipline-based Professor. Making Progress Even When Goals Don't Match', *Written Communication*, **18**, 180-228.

Grabe, W. and Kaplan, R. (1996) *Theory and Practice of Writing: An Applied Linguistic Perspective*, Longman: London.

Grobe, C. (1981) 'Syntactic Maturity, Mechanics, and Vocabulary as Predictors of Quality Ratings', *Research in the Teaching of English*, **15**, 1, 75-85.

Herrington, A. (1985) 'Writing in Academic Settings: A Study of the Contexts for Writing in Two Chemical Engineering Courses', *Research in the Teaching of English*,

19, 331-359.

Herrington, A. (1992) 'Composing One's Self in a Discipline: Students' and Teachers' Negotiations', in M. Secor and D. Charney (eds.), *Constructing Rhetorical Education*, 91-115, Southern Illinois University Press: Carbondale, IL.

Hilgers, T., Hussey, E. and Stitt-Bergh, M. (1999) 'As You're Writing, You Have These Epiphanies: What College Students Say about Writing and Learning in Their Majors', *Written Communication*, **16**, 317-353.

Hoffmann, A. (1998) 'An Exploratory Study of Goal Setting and the Nature of Articulated Goals in Second Language Writing Development', *New Zealand Studies in Applied Linguistics*, **4**, 33–48.

Johns, A. (1992) 'Toward Developing a Cultural Repertoire: A Case Study of a Lao College Freshman', in D. E. Murray (ed.), *Diversity as Resource: Redefining Cultural Literacy*, 183-198, Teachers of English to Speakers of Other Languages: Alexandria, VA.

John-Steiner, V. and Meehan, T. (2001) 'Creativity and Collaboration in Knowledge Construction', in C. D. Lee and P. Smagorinsky (eds.), *Vygotskian Perspectives on Literacy Research: Constructing Meaning Through Collaborative Inquiry*, 31-48, Cambridge University Press: Cambridge.

Kirkpatrick, A. (1997) 'Traditional Chinese Text Structures and Their Influence on the Writing in Chinese and English of Contemporary Mainland Chinese Students', *Journal of Second Language Writing*, **6**, 223-244.

Kubota, R. (1997) 'A Reevaluation of the Uniqueness of Japanese Written Discourse', *Written Communication*, **14**, 460-480.

Lantolf, J. and Pavlenko, A. (1995) 'Sociocultural Theory and Second Language Acquisition', *Annual Review of Applied Linguistics*, **15**, 108-124.

Lee, C. (2000) 'Signifying in the Zone of Proximal Development', in C. Lee and P. Smagorinsky (eds.), *Vygotskian Perspectives on Literacy Research: Constructing Meaning through Collaborative Inquiry*, 191-225, Cambridge University Press: Cambridge.

Leki, I. (1995) 'Coping Strategies of ESL Students in Writing Tasks across the Curriculum', *TESOL Quarterly*, **29**, 235-60.

Leki, I. 'Pretty Much I Screwed Up: Ill-served Needs of a Permanent Resident', in L. Harklau, K. Losey, and M. Siegal (eds.), *Generation 1.5 Meets College Composition: Issues in the Teaching of Writing to U.S –educated Learners of ESL*, 17-43, Lawrence Erlbaum Associates: Mahwah, NJ.

Leki, I. (2001) 'Hearing voices: L2 students' experiences in L2 writing courses', in T. Silva and P. K. Matsuda (eds.), *On second language writing*, 17-28, Lawrence Erlbaum Associates: Mahwah, NJ.

Leki, I. (2003) 'Living through college literacy: Nursing in a second language', *Written Communication*, **20**, 81-98.

Leki, I. and Carson, J. (1997) 'Completely Different Worlds: EAP and the Writing Experiences of ESL Students in University Courses', *TESOL Quarterly*, **31**, 39-69.

Leont'ev, A. (1978) *Activity, Consciousness and Personality*, Prentice Hall: Englewood Cliffs, NJ.

Leont'ev, A. (1981) 'The Problem of Activity in Psychology', in J. V. Wertsch (ed. and trans.), *The Concept of Activity in Soviet Psychology*, 37-71, M. E. Sharpe: New York.

Li, X. (1996) *"Good writing" in Cross-cultural Context*, State University of New York Press: Albany, NY.

McCarthy, L. (1987) 'A Stranger in Strange Lands: A College Student Writing across the Curriculum', *Research in the Teaching of English*, **21**, 233-265.

Miles, M. and Huberman, M. (1994) *Qualitative Data Analysis; An Expanded Sourcebook*, 2nd ed., CA: Sage, Thousand Oaks.

National Institute for Japanese Language, *Yutakana Fengoseikatsu No Tameni* [For a Rich and Expressive Language Life] (2002) Ministry of Finance of Japan, Tokyo.

Prior, P. (1998) *Writing/disciplinarity: A Sociohistoric Account of Literate Activity in the Academy*, Lawrence Erlbaum Associates: Mahwah, NJ.

Riazi, A. (1997) 'Acquiring Disciplinary Literacy: A Social-cognitive Analysis of Text Production and Learning among Iranian Graduate Students of Education', *Journal of Second Language Writing*, **6**, 105-137.

Schneider, M. and Fujishima, N. (1995) 'When Practice Doesn't Make Perfect: The Case of a Graduate ESL Student', in D. Belcher and G. Braine (eds.), *Academic writing in a second language: Essays on research and pedagogy*, 3-22, Ablex: Norwood, NJ.

Silva, T. (1992) 'L1 vs. L2 Writing: ESL Graduate Students' Perceptions', *TESL Canada Journal*, **10**, 27-47.

Spack, R. (1997) 'The Acquisition of Academic Literacy in a Second Language: A Longitudinal Case Study', *Written Communication*, **14**, 3-62.

Sternglass, M. (1997) *Time to Know Them: A Longitudinal Study of Writing and Learning at the College Level*, Lawrence Erlbaum Associates: Mahwah, NJ.

Vygotsky, L. (1978) *Mind in Society: The Development of Higher Psychological Processes*, Harvard University Press: Cambridge, MA.

Walvoord, B. and McCarthy, L. (1990) *Thinking and Writing in College: A Naturalistic Study of Students in Four Disciplines*, National Council of Teachers of English: Urbana, IL.

Wertsch, J. (1985) 'The Social Origins of Higher Mental Functions', in J.V. Wertsch (Ed.), *Vygotsky and the Social Formation of Mind*, 58-76, Harvard University Press: Cambridge, MA.

SCALING CHANGES IN LEARNERS' GOALS FOR WRITING IMPROVEMENT OVER AN ESL COURSE

Alister Cumming, Keanre Eouanzoui, Guillaume Gentil, and Luxin Yang

ABSTRACT

We interviewed, near the beginning and end of a pre-university ESL program, 45 students about their goals for writing improvement. We coded then plotted with Dual Scaling the goals expressed in both interviews in terms of long-term aspirations, objects of goals, and actions taken to achieve goals. These aspects of the goals were mentioned with similar frequencies, and they clustered together in similar ways, between the first and second interviews. We conclude that the students' goals for ESL writing improvement and patterns of individual difference in them remained relatively stable over the duration of the ESL course.

Introduction

Among the many recent studies of writing in second languages, longitudinal case studies have provided some of the most compelling insights into students' learning processes (Cumming 2001: 7). Indeed, documenting the long-term changes that occur naturally in students' language production is perhaps the optimal method for research to identify trends in second language acquisition and writing achievement (Hillocks 1986; Little, Schnabel and Baumert 2000; Mellow, Reeder and Forster 1996). Nonetheless, the types of evidence and the units of analyses employed in such inquiry can vary greatly, even within the domain of second-language writing. For example, some studies have focused on changes in functional dimensions of the texts that students produce (e.g. Albrechtsen 1997; Nassaji and Cumming 2000). Other studies have drawn mainly on interviews and observational data to depict the progressive development of a single student's writing and personal sense of identity in relation to the literate contexts for using the second language that the person has encountered (e.g. Buckwalter and Lo 2002; Spack 1997). Other researchers have traced the effects of a specific pedagogical approach on groups of students' writing and knowledge over the duration of a course (e.g. Donato and McCormick 1994; Yeh 1998).

A common purpose in these various studies has been to identify the changes that are most salient in naturally-occurring cases of second-language writing development then to interpret those changes in respect to the personal characteristics of, and social contexts experienced by, individual students. Pursuing such a purpose as well in the present study[1], we opted for a unique focus of analysis: to identify changes in the goals that a group of adult students expressed—during interviews at the beginning then at the end of an intensive, pre-university ESL (English as a Second Language) program—for improving their writing in English. And we opted for an innovative method of statistical analysis: dual-scaling, an approach to analyzing symmetrical relations among categorical data developed by Nishisato (1994), akin to principal components analysis but without requiring the logical assumptions of inferential statistics (Nishisato and Nishisato 1983, 1994). Our focus on goals for writing improvement is informed by activity theory (Leont'ev 1979; see article by Yang, Baba and Cumming, this volume) and goal theory (e.g. Austin and Vancouver 1996). Our choice of dual scaling arose because we want to account for the complexity of factors inherent in second-language writing development while recognizing that the variability among the relatively small number of culturally and linguistically diverse students in our sample population entails multiple interactions that we could not adequately evaluate by conventional statistics or without a strict experimental design (Cumming and Riazi 2000).

The analyses reported in the present article are from the first year of a two-year, longitudinal study. We aimed to determine whether students participating in our study changed their goals for writing improvement between the beginning and the end of a three-month ESL program designed to prepare themselves for university studies the following year. As such, the present analyses are preliminary to more extensive analyses we are now doing with additional, parallel data we have collected from 15 of these students during their first year of university studies (in the year following the data reported here).

Method

Participants
We solicited 45 volunteer students from 8 classes in an academic preparation ESL program at a university in Toronto. Their backgrounds are outlined in Appendix A. The students came from a variety of cultural and linguistic backgrounds, the largest numbers being from China (14) and Korea (7), smaller numbers from Iran (4), Japan (3), Thailand (3), Israel (3), Mexico (3), Vietnam (2), and Morocco (2), and single students from Chile, Ecuador, Saudi Arabia, and Ukraine. There were 34 females and 11 males. Most (i.e. 30) of the students were between 18 and 23, another 12 were between 24 and 30,

and 3 were between 31 and 36. Slightly more than half had only high school degrees or a few years of college or university studies, whereas the others had Bachelor's or post-graduate degrees, as shown in Appendix A. Most (i.e. 28) had been in Canada for less than 6 months at the time of their first interviews, whereas the others had been in Canada for a half-year or more. The classes they were taking were designated either 'high intermediate' or 'advanced', so the students were relatively proficient in English. Their average score on the TOEFL (Test of English as a Foreign Language) was 550, which is commonly a requirement for university entrance in North America.

Data Collection
We interviewed and audio-taped each participant twice, first shortly after the beginning of their course, then a second time about 6 weeks later, near the end of the course (in the academic year 2001-2002). Each interview was conducted individually for about one hour using the same standard interview schedule (which we had elaborated from a pilot study described in Cumming, Busch and Zhou 2002). The interviewer asked the students to describe various aspects of their goals for writing improvement, starting with general questions (e.g. What goals do you have for improving your writing in English at university?) then more specific questions (e.g. Are you trying to improve your grammar in your writing? What grammar would you like to improve? How are you doing this? Please give examples). Next, the students were asked to produce stimulated recalls of a piece of writing they had produced for their ESL course, indicating their specific goals and composing processes for writing the piece.

Analyses
We transcribed the interviews in full then coded the transcripts with NVivo, a software package for qualitative data analyses, using a typology of goals that we developed and refined through various iterations until we established levels of inter-coder agreement of between 75% and 85% (described in Cumming 2002). We tallied the frequency of occurrence for each goal category then analyzed through Dual 3 (stastical software series, Nishisato and Nishisato, 1983) the distribution of the frequencies of the students' goals per category, per student, and per interview. Although dual scaling produces multiple solutions to any data analysis, for reasons of parsimony we present below only plots of solution 1 versus solution 2, considering this to approximate an optimal representation of our data matrices.[2]

The dual-scaled data provide a kind of map showing the relative distance between each student and each goal category for each interview, this distance being a function of the number of times each student expressed each goal category during each interview. That is, the closer a student is to a goal category, the greater the number of times he or she had expressed this particular goal category during the interview. Furthermore, the analyses represent the distance between a student and a particular goal category for each of the two interviews. That is, if a student expressed one goal category a great number of times in both interviews, he or she mapped on the graph close to this category for both interviews. Alternatively, if this student expressed the goal category frequently in the first interview then seldom in the second interview, then that person mapped close to this category for the first interview but far from the category in the second interview. In this way, the plotted graphs from the dual scaling analyses help to identify consistencies or changes in the students' responses across interviews in terms of the relative distance between the categorical responses in the first interview and those in the second interview. These analyses are essentially exploratory, however, in the sense that we have had to interpret the patterns we perceive in the plotted graphs in order to make sense of the data they display.

For the present analyses we selected only three of the goal categories that we coded in the interview data, primarily for ease of interpretation and because these categories are the most generally meaningful. The first of these categories is the long-term **aspirations** that students expressed for improving their ESL writing, which we categorized as referring either to preparation for university studies, one's future career or work, or specific English proficiency tests. The second category is the **objects** of each goal that the students expressed. We coded these as referring to either language (i.e. grammar and vocabulary), rhetoric or genres, composing processes, ideas and knowledge, affective states, learning and transfer, or identity. The third category we analyzed here were the **actions** the students said they took to achieve their goals, which we classified as either seeking assistance from teachers, seeking assistance from other people, using self-regulation or heuristics, using tools or resources, studying, altering their conditions for writing, or reading. The exact frequencies that each of these goal categories was mentioned in the interviews are documented in Cumming (2002)[3].

Findings

Aspirations
The most frequent, long-term aspirations cited in the students' descriptions of their goals for ESL writing improvement concerned their intended

university studies (over half of the aspirations expressed) and career plans (more than a third of the aspirations expressed). A few students (about 10%) also related their ESL writing goals to test preparation, notably the TOEFL, presumably because scores on this test are a common requirement for entrance to universities in North America. The total frequencies of these sub-categories of aspirations changed little from the first to the second set of interviews.

For instance, in the following excerpt from her second interview, Sara described (in response to a question about specific types of writing) her intention to improve her abilities with certain text types in order to prepare herself for university studies:

> I have to.. um, I should be .. prepare for university because in university, I need some essays and research, so I should uh.. attend to the.. work on them and actually I have um.. I'm trying to now, for example, inference of data, how to summary something or how to research. Or if I have project, how to work on that. I think these are the most important that I have to work on them and try to progress and advance on them.

In her first interview, Sara related her goals for ESL improvement to both her intended academic studies and her future career needs:

> I trying to improve my essays as well because essays is .. Now, in my course that I take is important how should I write the essays. And maybe it's useful for my future as well because it has connected with my future, I think. So, letters [...] maybe formal letters or something like resume. Yeah. I should improve that [...] for university, job or other thing. Ya. They are useful, but.. Stories, I don't think.

The dual-scaled graph in Figure 1 provides a two-dimensional representation of the distribution of the frequencies of answers per student, aspiration type, and interview number. The two axes are the first two solutions of the equation optimizing the between-row (students) and between-column (aspiration variables) discrimination as well as the relation between responses weighted by row weights and those by column weights. Together, the first two solutions represent 61% of the variability in these data. The categories of responses are identified with triangles, the students with circles. Hong, for instance, expressed university-related aspirations 4 times in the first interview, then 7 times in the second interview; by contrast, she never expressed test-related aspirations, and she expressed career-related aspirations only twice in each

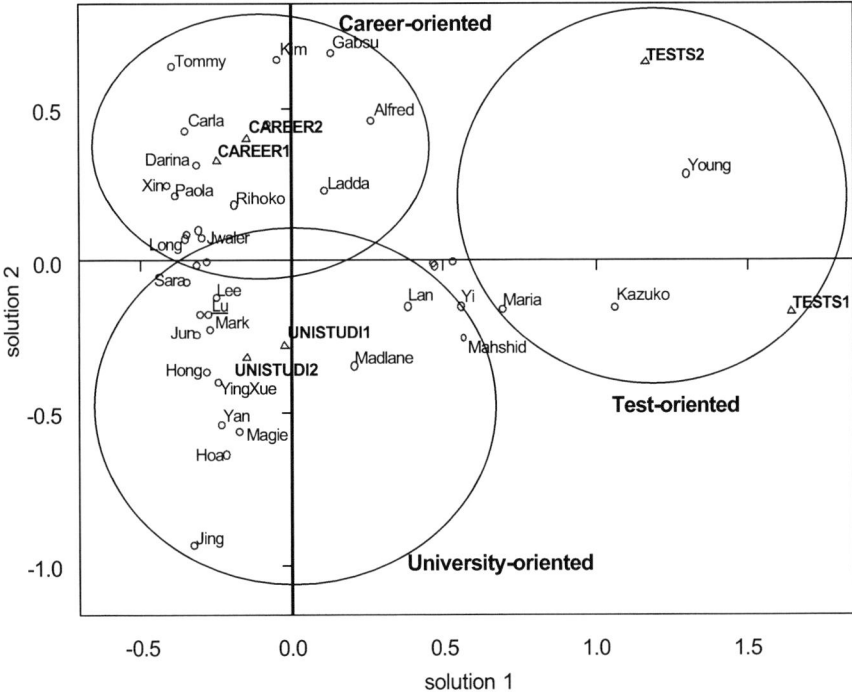

Figure 1. Aspirations in interviews 1 and 2

interview. Therefore, she mapped close to University Studies, away from Career, and further away from Test. The number next to the variables' names refers to the interview number. That is, Career1, University1, and Test1 represent the students' responses in the first interviews, and Career2, University2, and Test2 their answers in the second interviews.

In Figure 1 most of the students map onto the western hemisphere close to the career and university variables. These two variables together represent close to 90% of the students' statements about their aspirations. The circles that we have inserted into Figure 1 identify three groups of students: a career-oriented group in the north-west quadrant, a university-oriented group in the south-west quadrant, and a test-oriented group in the eastern hemisphere. Some students such as Sara map between groups, reflecting the equivalency of their answers in two or three of the aspiration categories. Most of the students who expressed aspirations related to tests also expressed university-related aspirations more frequently than career-related aspirations and therefore map onto the southern hemisphere.

For each category of aspirations, the responses to the first interviews map closely to the responses in the second interviews. That is, Career1 and Career2 map closely to each other in the same quadrant, and so do University1 and University2. Although further apart, Test1 and Test2 map in the same zone on the far-end of the eastern hemisphere. Furthermore, the relatively greater distance between Test1 and Test2 compared to the other response categories can be explained by the smaller frequencies of responses in these categories (less than 10%). On the whole, the proximity of first-interview responses to second-interview responses in each category suggests that the students tend to give similar answers across interviews. For this reason, we conclude that the students did not shift their focus from one kind of aspirations to another between the first and second interviews.

Objects

Among the objects on which the students said they focused their goals for ESL writing improvement, language-related goals were the most frequent (35% of goal statements), focusing mostly on vocabulary (e.g. 'I want to improve my vocabulary'), grammar (e.g. 'to improve my grammar.') or particular elements of language (e.g. articles, conjunctions, transition words). Rhetorical structures and genres were the second most frequently cited

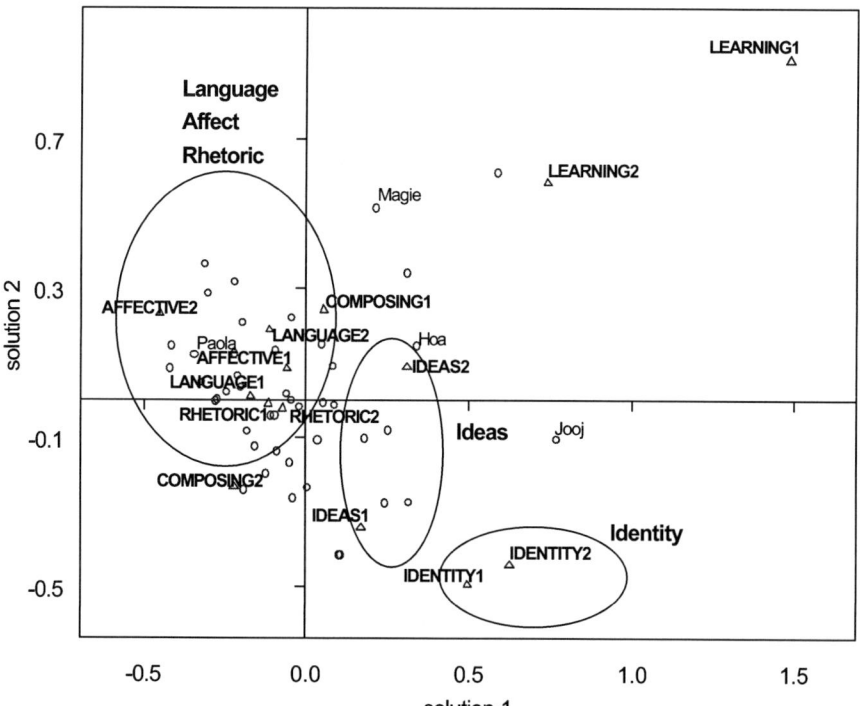

Figure 2. Objects in interviews 1 and 2

objects of goals (27% of goal statements), including, for example, essay writing, résumés, and research articles. The third most frequently mentioned objects were ideas and knowledge (21% of the goal statements), particularly to develop concepts and arguments expressed in their writing. This was followed by composing processes (7%) (e.g, 'I never write anything without an outline. I'm trying to improve this.'). Goals related to affective states (i.e. changing one's emotional disposition to writing and improving one's confidence as a writer) and to identity (i.e. finding one's own style and expressing oneself in writing) appeared infrequently (about 4% each). Goals related to learning and transfer were rare (less than 2%), referring to the activities pursued by learners for the purpose of transforming their knowledge and skills or transferring them to other courses. Sometimes, the students described two or more objects for their goals simultaneously. For instance, Magie stated that she wanted to learn a writing 'strategy to organize her ideas' more effectively.

Figure 2 shows the students' objects of goals for the first two dual scaling solutions, representing 32% of the variability in these data. Most of the students cluster around the four most frequently cited objects of goals: language, rhetoric, ideas, and composing. Furthermore, two main clusters can be identified, as indicated by the circles we have inserted into Figure 2. One group of students—predominantly concerned about language, affective states, and rhetoric—cluster in the western hemisphere. Within this group, there appears to be a rhetoric-focused sub-group in the south-west quadrant and a language-focused sub-group in the north-west quadrant. The proximity between the affective and language objects in the latter quadrant reflects a tendency for students to mention these two types of objects together. This tendency is exemplified in the following excerpts from Paola's interviews, which also show her identifying a goal in the form of a dilemma in the first interview then moving toward a resolution of the dilemma in the second interview:

> (Interview 1): By now I don't feel so confident, because it's not my, I'm not so freely in the writing, sometimes I need, I think I need more time to write in English. And sometimes I feel frustrated, because (...) in Spanish I have to just think about the ideas, now I have to think about ideas, grammatical order, articles, conjunctions, like I have to think more, like to think twice. So by now I don't feel so confident.
>
> (Interview 2): right now I feel better. I feel very confident when I write. I feel that, I have improved my vocabulary, not so much, how I would like, but it's better than before.

A second, more disparate cluster of students appears in the eastern hemisphere around the ideas variables. Two smaller subgroups of outlying students also appear in the eastern hemisphere: A few students mapped closely to the identity variable in the south east quadrant, and a couple of other students mapped closely to learning and transfer in the north-east quadrant. These patterns indicate that only a few students expressed concerns over these aspects of their goals for writing improvement.

There were remarkably few shifts in the students' expressed objects of goals from the first to the second interviews. However, one notable exception concerns the variables of ideas and of composing. Composing moved from the north-east to the south-west quadrant. Ideas moved in the opposite direction (from the south-east to the north-east quadrant). Evidently, some students expressed more composing-related goals in their first interviews, then more ideas-related goals in their second interviews, whereas other students showed a reverse pattern. This tendency may have several explanations. It may reflect differences in the emphases of the five different instructors that taught the students. Or, it could be that some students accomplished certain goals during their course then shifted to different goals by the time of the second interview. Or this pattern could be an artefact of the interview technique, if some students talked less in the second interview about the objects of goals that they had already described in detail in the first interview, assuming the interviewer already knew about the former goals. Nonetheless, the overall pattern in this analysis is one of consistency: Students tended to express the same objects of their goals for improving their ESL writing in both interviews.

Actions taken

Studying, seeking teachers' assistance, and use of resources (such as dictionaries) were the three actions most frequently mentioned by students, totalling over 70% of the students' statements about their goals. Other actions taken included reading (e.g. 'I try to improve my vocabulary in my writing by reading a lot of short articles on the CBC Web site'), seeking other people's assistance (e.g. 'I don't like the grammar checker but other people check for me'), and uses of self-regulation or heuristics, as in this excerpt from Sharon's first interview:

> How I am trying to improve? I'm just trying […] to give a lot of attention when I have my homework. And to give attention for vocabulary choices. I am really, I have time at home to think about the words. How I want to… […] the essay or the sentence how I want to write it. So write what I want. Exactly what I want.

And that will be right. I'm doing it um... I'm just giving it more time than usual [...] to think about it. To.. kind of teach myself thinking to write.

Only rarely (in 4% of their goal statements) did students mention altering their conditions for writing to change the material conditions of their learning, for example, by using Internet chat rooms, drinking coffee, or seeking out opportunities for non-traditional educational activities.

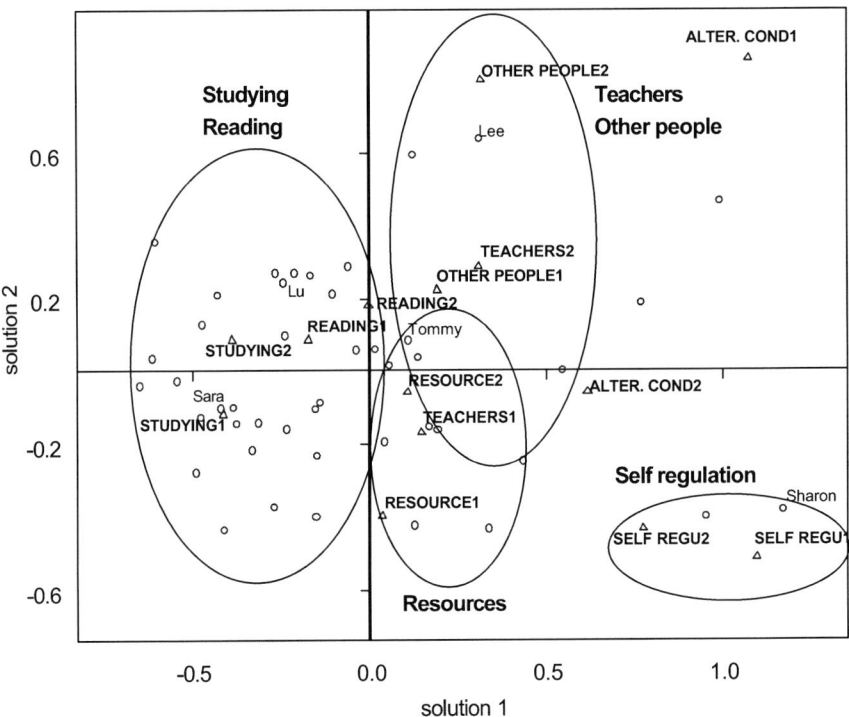

Figure 3. Actions in interviews 1 and 2

Figure 3 shows the first two solutions of dual scaling, representing 43% of the variability in these data, the actions that the students said they took to achieve their writing goals. Three main groups appear, as indicated by the circles we have inserted to Figure 3. A studying and reading group is in the western hemisphere. A group that frequently cited seeking assistance from their teachers and from others appears in the north-east quadrant and in the north-west part of the south-east quadrant. A group that frequently mentioned using resources and self-regulation appears in the south-east quadrant. These groupings suggest different preferred learning styles: reliance on teachers and other people, reliance on self and resources, or reliance on studying and reading. However, the proximity of resources and teachers' assistance may indicate that the students who relied on their teachers for help with their writing also tended to use resources such as dictionaries and grammar books. Importantly, there was almost no shift between the first and second interviews, suggesting that the students did not markedly change the actions they took to achieve their goals for ESL writing improvement over the duration of their ESL writing courses.

Discussion

The overall result emerging from these analyses is that the 45 students we interviewed tended to describe their long-term aspirations, the objects of their goals, and the actions they took to achieve their goals for ESL writing improvement in fundamentally similar ways and in similar frequencies near the beginning and near the end of their ESL program. This finding confirms the consistency of these goals and of the responses elicited by our interview schedule. ESL students may not alter their goals for writing improvement very much during one course. Presumably, people tend to retain their long-term aspirations once they are established. The goals associated with ESL writing improvement may take a relatively long time to achieve because they include many complex aspects of language, rhetoric, and self-image. Likewise, the actions that students come to adopt in a course may suffice to fulfil their purposes for learning in that context. As Engeström (1991) observed, learning in academic contexts tends to be relatively encapsulated, and not susceptible to radical changes.

The dual scaling analyses point out some interesting patterns in these students' conceptualizations of their goals for writing improvement. In terms of long-term aspirations for writing improvement, we have distinguished students who may be motivated differently by goals related to writing that they expect to do in university courses, writing they expect to do in their future careers, or writing they expect to do for English proficiency tests. Likewise, there appear to be relations among the objects on which ESL students focus their goals for writing improvement. Certain students expressed emotional attitudes related to their concerns for grammar, vocabulary, and rhetoric in their writing in English. Others shifted between a focus on composing processes and on ideas as their courses progressed. Only a small number of students were aware of trying to develop a unique identity while writing in English. Thirdly, the actions that these ESL students said they took to achieve their goals for writing improvement tended to reflect particular learning styles, for example, with some students relying often on assistance from teachers and others, other students being more self-reliant and using resources such as dictionaries or computers, and others being studious and using reading to model their writing. These analyses, nonetheless, are exploratory and descriptive only, and do not involve any methods of evaluating whether any of these clusters of variables may be more or less effective for learning to write in English, even among this small group of ESL learners from a variety of different cultural and linguistic backgrounds.

The present analyses set a foundation for complementary analyses we are now conducting to compare qualities of the goals expressed during the ESL program with goals for writing improvement that a subset of these students expressed, a year later, in the context of studying academic courses at university. We expect that the change in educational context, the unique demands for writing in particular courses and disciplines, and the time difference of a full year should produce certain changes in these students' goals for writing improvement in English. But until our next set of analyses are completed it is difficult to predict what these changes might be, other than to suggest that they should be of interest to educators designing and teaching ESL academic preparation courses. Dual scaling has proved to be an appropriate tool for analyzing these data, accounting for the complex relations among variables and individual students while plotting changes that may appear, or not appear, over time.

Notes

[1] We gratefully acknowledge funding for this research through grant 410-2001-0791 from the Social Sciences and Humanities Research Council of Canada to Alister Cumming. We thank the participating students and teachers as well other members of the research team working on this project, who assisted in developing the research instruments and various aspects of data collection and analysis: Kyoko Baba, Michael Busch, Jill Cummings, Usman Erdosy, Cheryl Fretz, Tae-Young Kim, and Ally Zhou.

[2] The solutions in dual scaling are, for categorical data, akin to the components in principal components analysis for numerical data. The number of solutions depends upon the type of categorical data. In the case of frequency tables, the total number of solutions is the smaller number out of the number of rows (say, n) and columns (say, m) minus one (i.e. minimum {n, m} – 1), giving rise to the number of solutions taken in combinations of two at a time to produce a graphical display, as in Figures 1, 2, and 3. That is, for a 45-by-6 contingency table, the total number of solutions is 5 and the corresponding total combinations of two solutions is 10

$$(\text{or } \frac{number\_solutions \times (number\_solutions - 1)}{2})$$

³ The other goal categories that we coded in the interview data, but which are not discussed in the present article were the **force** of the goal, the **context** of the actions taken, the **origins** of the goal, and the **responsibility** cited for the goal. Our dual scaling analyses showed that none of these categories altered much between the first and second interviews.

References

Albrechtsen, D. (1997) 'A Discourse Analysis of Narrative Essays Written in English by Danish Students', in K. Pogner (ed.), *Writing: Text and Interaction, Odense Working Papers in Language and Communication*, 14, 1-40.

Austin, J. and Vancouver, J. (1996) 'Goal Constructs in Psychology: Structure, Process, and Content', *Psychological Bulletin*, 120, 338-375.

Buckwalter, J. and Lo, Y. (2002) 'Emergent Biliteracy in Chinese and English', *Journal of Second Language Writing*, 11, 4, 269-293.

Cumming, A. (2001) 'Learning to Write in a Second Language: Two Decades of Research', in R. Manchon (ed.), *International Journal of English Studies*, Special Issue, *Writing in the L2 Classroom: Issues in Research and Pedagogy*, 1, 2, 1-23.

Cumming, A. (2002) 'Should They Correspond? Goals for ESL Writing Improvement Among Adult Learners and Their Instructors', Paper presented at AILA's World Congress of Applied Linguistics, Singapore, December 19, 2002.

Cumming, A., Busch, M., and Zhou, A. (2002) 'Investigating Learners' Goals in the Context of Adult Second-language Writing', in G. Rijlaarsdam (Series ed.) and S. Ransdell and M. Barbier (Volume eds.), *Studies in Writing*, 11: *New Directions for Research in L2 Writing*, 189-208, Kluwer Academic: Dordrecht, The Netherlands.

Cumming, A. and Riazi, A. (2000) 'Building Models of Adult Second-language Writing Instruction', *Learning and Instruction*, 10, 55-71.

Donato, R. and McCormick, D. (1994) 'A Sociocultural Perspective on Language Learning Strategies: The Role of Mediation', *Modern Language Journal*, 78, 4, 453-464.

Engeström, Y. (1991) 'Overcoming the Encapsulation of School Learning', *Learning and Instruction*, 4, 243-259.

Hillocks, G. (1986) *Research on Written Composition: New Directions for Teaching*, ERIC Clearing House on Reading and Communication Skills: Urbana, Il.

Leont'ev, A. (1979) 'The Problem of Activity in Psychology', in J. V. Wertsch (ed. and trans.), *The Concept of Activity in Soviet Psychology*, 37-71, M. E. Sharpe: New York.

Little, T., Schnabel, K. and Baumert, J. (2000) (eds.) *Modeling Longitudinal and Multilevel Data*, Lawrence Erlbaum Associates: Mahwah, NJ.

Mellow, D., Reeder, K. and Forster, E. (1996) 'Using Time-Series Research Designs to Investigate the Effects of Instruction on SLA', *Studies in Second Language*

Acquisition, **18**, 3, 325-350.

Nassaji, H. and Cumming, A. (2000) 'What's in a ZPD? A Case Study of a Young ESL Student and Teacher Interacting Through Dialogue Journals', *Language Teaching Research*, **4**, 2, 95-121.

Nishisato, S. (1994) *Elements of Dual Scaling: An Introduction to Practical Data Analysis*, Lawrence Erlbaum Associates: Hillsdale, NJ.

Nishisato, S. and Nishisato, I. (1983) *DUAL 3: Statistical Software Series*, MicroStats: Toronto.

Nishisato, S. and Nishisato, I. (1994) *Dual Scaling in a Nutshell*, MicroStats: Toronto.

Spack, R. (1997) 'The Acquisition of Academic Literacy in a Second Language: A Longitudinal Case Study', *Written Communication*, **14**, 3-62.

Yeh, S. (1998) 'Empowering Education: Teaching Argumentative Writing to Cultural Minority Middle-School Students', *Research in the Teaching of English*, **33**, 1, 49-83.

Appendix A. Profile of Participants

Pseudonym	Gender	Age*	Country of Origin	L1	Prior Education and Work Experience*	Months in Canada*
Alfred	M	18-23	Israel	Arabic & Hebrew	High school	16
Boom Hee	F	18-23	Korea	Korean	High school	12
Carla	F	24-30	Chile	Spanish	B.A. (business)	4
Chulsu	M	24-30	Korea	Korean	B.A. (law/business)	3
Claudia	F	24-30	Mexico	Spanish	B.A. (business administration)	2
Darina	F	31-36	Ukraine	Russian & Ukrainian	M.D. (medicine), physician for 4 years	4
Gabsu	M	31-36	Korea	Korean	B.A. (economics), TV producer for 5 years	1
Gade	F	18-23	Thailand	Thai	B.Sc. (chemical engineering)	8
Hana	F	18-23	Japan	Japanese	High school	6
Hoa	F	18-23	Vietnam	Vietnamese	University for 1 year	8
Hong	F	31-36	China	Chinese	B.A. (advertising)	24
Jina	F	18-23	Korea	Korean	University student (business administration)	4
Jing	F	18-23	China	Chinese	University for 1 year	4
Jooj	F	18-23	Iran	Farsi	High school	6
Jun	M	18-23	China	Chinese	High school	7
Jwahar	F	18-23	Saudi Arabia	Arabic	High school	6
Kazuko	F	24-30	Japan	Japanese	University student for 2 years	16
Kim	M	24-30	Korea	Korean	B.A. (graphic design), software programmer	2

Ladda	F	24-30	Thailand	Thai	B.A. (Japanese), translator for 4 years	1
Lan	F	18-23	Vietnam	Vietnamese	High school	2
Lee	F	18-23	China	Chinese	High school	5
Long	M	18-23	China	Chinese	High school	5
Lu	F	18-23	China	Chinese	High school	5
Madlane	F	18-23	Israel	Arabic	B.Sc. (civil engineering)	5
Magie	F	18-23	Iran	Farsi	College for 2 years	7
Mahshid	F	18-23	Iran	Farsi	B.Sc.	21
Maria	F	18-23	Morocco	French	High school	1
Mark	M	18-23	China	Chinese	High school	12
Martha	F	24-30	Mexico	Spanish	B.A. (accounting), accountant for 1 year	1
Mehdi	M	18-23	Morocco	Arabic & French	College certificate, clerk for 6 months	34
Pam	F	24-30	Thailand	Thai	M.A. (economics), lending officer for 2 years	1
Paola	F	24-30	Ecuador	Spanish	B.A. (business), actuarial assistant for 2 years	4
Qing	M	18-23	China	Chinese	High school	12
Rihoko	F	18-23	Japan	Japanese	High school	18
Sara	F	18-23	Iran	Farsi	High school	5
Sharon	F	18-23	Israel (born in Russia)	Hebrew	High school	2
Sumi	F	24-30	Korea	Korean	B.A. (architectural engineering)	1
Tommy	M	24-30	Mexico	Spanish	B.A. (architecture)	6
Wenzhen	F	18-23	China	Chinese	High school	9
Wu-long	M	24-30	China	Chinese	College certificate (business), financial advisor for 6 years	5
Xin	F	18-23	China	Chinese	High school	9

*Age, prior education, work experience, and months of residence in Canada are reported here from the first interview. Work experience is indicated only for students who had such experience (i.e. most did not).

ATTENTION TO ARGUMENTATION IN LEARNER TEXT PRODUCTION: HOW DO WE CAPTURE LEARNER ABILITY IN ARGUMENTATION?

Dorte Albrechtsen, Kirsten Haastrup and Birgit Henriksen

ABSTRACT

The article addresses the assumption that verbal reports produced by foreign language learners while engaged on a restricted writing task can supply information on their ability to argue in writing that might not be captured in verbal protocols produced while writing essays. We report on analyses of the protocols of five students at three educational levels. In the restricted writing task, the processing demands are reduced in that the learners are given start and end sentences and are only required to select a number of sentences from a supplied list in order to produce a short text. Comparing how the learners perform on the two tasks, we conclude that the restricted writing task might indeed provide us with useful information on learner development in argumentative writing.

Introduction

This article reports on work which is part of an ongoing project *Processes in writing and vocabulary acquisition in English as a foreign language*.[1] The overall aim of the project is to trace the development of, and possible interactions between, writing processes, lexical guessing strategies and various aspects of vocabulary knowledge in learners of a foreign language at three educational levels in a within-subjects design. This development is also being investigated with respect to the learners' processing ability and knowledge of vocabulary in their mother tongue. The present paper deals with the writing component of the project.

To ensure that development could be traced in learner groups of different age and maturational levels, it was clearly necessary to focus on development in writing in relation to argumentative text production. We know from research in L1 and L2 composition that the argumentative genre is a cognitively highly demanding mode, as is demonstrated by the fact that competence in this mode is acquired fairly late – if at all – in the population at large (see, for example, Freedman and Pringle 1989; Kuhn 1991).

Let us start by addressing the matter of the demands and constraints posed by argumentative text production and we shall then follow this by a description of the types of data that we have collected. In answering the question of how best to capture differences in learners' abilities in argumentation, we aim to assess the degree to which a more restricted writing task can prove a useful supplement to the freer task of essay writing. With a view to answering this question, the final portion of this paper will be devoted to discussions of results from a sub-set of informants from the three educational levels mentioned above.

Argumentative text production

What do learners need to be able to write an argumentative text? They clearly require *knowledge* of argumentation and good *writing skills* – here understood as processing flexibility. The necessary knowledge takes the form of familiarity with the rules of argumentation backed by general textual knowledge. The minimum requirements are ability to present a point of view and to produce supporting arguments. Extended argumentation calls for the learner to realise why one argues in the first place. Here the absence of an interlocutor poses a real problem, inasmuch as the writer has to imagine an opponent's view in order to be able to operate with counter-arguments. With regard to writing skills, writers need to use an approach that ensures that they have sufficient processing capacity to attend to a number of factors: 1) deciding on own point of view; 2) deciding on the point of view of the opponent; 3) selecting arguments in support of one's own view, and arguments in support of the view of the opponent, plus selecting arguments that refute those supporting the opponent's position, which in turn will strengthen the writer's own position; 4) generating ideas and 5) converting ideas and the hierarchical representation of the argumentation structure into a linear presentation in the text itself. This last point naturally poses extra problems for the learner writing in a foreign language.

The written product will reveal the result of this combination of knowledge and processing. As is known from verbal protocol analysis, much more is involved in the act of writing than is ever to be found in the final product. When trying to trace development, one is naturally interested in establishing the degree to which a particular learner lacks sufficient knowledge and/or processing capacity to be able to write in this mode, and also in pinpointing the stages along the way to the ultimate goal. If the product satisfies the requirements of the genre, then it can be assumed that the goal has been reached, in the sense that the writer possesses the knowledge and processing skills required. If, on the other hand, the product fails to satisfy the requirements, one needs to discover whether the learner possesses the relevant knowledge but lacks processing capacity to demonstrate his/her knowledge in the product; or alternatively, if the learner has the processing capacity but lacks the knowledge needed to produce an argumentative text.

With regard to writing skills, a number of studies dealing with the writing process in L1 and L2 have investigated the differences between good and poor writers through the use of verbal protocols (e.g. Cumming 1989; Cumming 1990; Whalen and Ménard 1995; Roca de Larios et al. 2001). The work we report on here tries to account for good and poor writing processes by analysing the types of problem solving the informants carry out while in the process of writing. It is known that verbal protocols can only reveal parts of the story, since learners only verbalise what they are attending to at any given moment (Ericsson and Simon 1993). They might therefore not reveal everything that is going on in their minds, but this is the best that can be achieved short of having direct access to their mental operations.

We might cherish a hope that learners' verbalisations would disclose knowledge of argumentation, even though the essay produced shows no evidence of any such knowledge. In other words, do verbalisations in fact reveal how learners decide on their own point of view and on an opposing point of view? Do they indicate that learners consider the pros and cons of the case, and how to present a line of argument? The answers to these questions will again depend on whether or not the learners attend to these issues at a certain point in the production process. That is to say, they may simultaneously be focussing on other matters, and thus the competition for attention might result in leaving considerations in relation to argumentation non-verbalised. Therefore, we need to look for other ways of gaining access to the learners' state of knowledge of argumentation; one such possibility is to use a more restricted writing exercise, for example, what is known as the 'alpha-omega task'.

The alpha-omega task – a simulation
Since learners have to attend to so many factors at the same time, it is difficult to capture learners' ability to produce argumentative texts in free text production. Consequently a group of researchers from France and Holland (Andriessen et al. 1996; Coirier et al. 1999) decided to work on ways of experimentally isolating some of the factors involved in producing argumentative texts. These researchers described these factors as a number of constraints that had to be met for the production of an elaborated argumentative text. Four of the constraints are preconditions for argumentation to occur in the first place, namely:
- recognising a conflict of opinion;
- recognising the topic as debatable (socially, ideologically and contextually);

- accepting that the conflict can be solved;
- accepting that the solution can be reached by means of language.

The other four constraints relate more directly to the actual production of the text:
- being prepared to take a stand on the issue;
- providing support for the claim;
- acknowledging the opposite claim and support for that claim;
- refuting the opposite claim by means of counter-argumentation.

The experimental task, used by the research group, isolates the planning of argumentative and thematic coherence, under the assumption that the four preconditions are met through the way in which the task is devised; while the other four conditions are satisfied by the manner in which the learners solve the task. In the alpha-omega task, students are given start and end sentences (e.g. *It is nice to live in a city* and *That's why it is better to live in a village*). From a set of 24 available possibilities, students have to pick out six sentences to be inserted between the start and the end sentences with the aim of creating a coherent text. Since idea generation, formulation of these ideas and the identification of the opponent's point of view have all been taken care of, this type of task significantly reduces the writers' processing load – the learners simply have to choose appropriate sentences. In so doing, the learners need to assess each sentence in relation to thematisation and argumentative orientation. If the learner complies with both argumentative and textual constraints, the optimal text can be described in the manner illustrated in Figure 1.

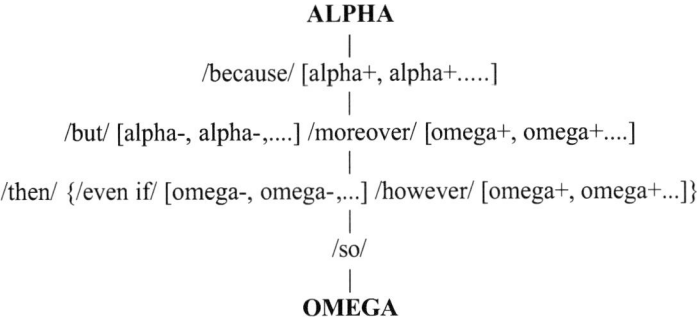

Figure 1. Textual structure of the alpha-omega task that complies with argumentative and textual requirements (Source: Coirier et al. 1999: 24)

The alpha-omega paradigm involves scoring the texts produced by the learners. For this assessment, the researchers devised a scoring system that took account not only of thematisation but also argumentative orientation. The task was presented to a total of 578 learners in slightly different versions. The participants (aged 10-14 years) all solved the task in their L1. Coirier et al. (1999) collated the results from all these experiments, finding that only 6.4 percent of their population could be characterised as 'experts'. Because the alpha-omega task has been so thoroughly investigated, it was decided to include it in our own research design, partly to serve as an additional writing task to give to the informants, and partly as a means of capturing differences in learners' ability to argue in writing. It is the latter function that will form the focus of this paper. In what follows, an attempt will be made to answer the question: to what extent can the alpha-omega task reveal attention to argumentation that is not clear from the essay writing task?

Data from the present study

At the outset, the informants were screened so as ensure that those who were enrolled to take part in the study had the ability to use 'think aloud' procedures. This screening also served as a form of training for the participants in these techniques. In addition, all informants watched extracts from video recordings of a student verbalising while writing an essay in Danish and English. The participants were explicitly told that the choice of L1 or L2 for verbalising was entirely up to them.

For the collection of verbal protocols, the informants were seated in a university language laboratory, using only alternate booths so as to ensure that the informants did not disturb one another. This set-up meant that several informants could be tested simultaneously, thus minimising the subject/researcher interaction found in other situations of data collection in which informants and researchers are in much closer contact (see for example Smagorinsky 1994; Jourdenais 2001). In our project, the sole prompting given to the informants during the tasks was merely for research assistants to point unobtrusively to a sign reminding participants to verbalise. Even this was resorted to only if it appeared that informants were not actually moving their lips. It is possible to state with confidence that the informants who took part in this study verbalised willingly and continuously.

The informants wrote two argumentative essays, one in Danish and one in English, while verbalising their thoughts. Writing prompts were taken from the TOEFL list. Time on task was 90 minutes for each essay. The participants were also required to undertake the alpha-omega task, again in both languages while verbalising concurrently. Prompts for this task were taken from Andriessen et al. (1996), together with the addition of others devised especially for this project. As stated above, Andriessen and colleagues had experimented with different versions of the task, but the form chosen for our study was that which in their research had seemed least likely to place constraints on the investigation. Hence, so as to ensure that a specific point of view was not imposed upon them, the informants were asked to choose which one of *two* combinations of start and end sentences they wished to employ – for example, either: (start) *It is nice to live in a village* + (end) *That is why it is better to live in a city*; or (start) *It is nice to live in a city* + (end) *That is why it is better to live in a village*. The participants' task was to produce a short coherent text on the basis of 24 pre-set sentences. As recommended by Coirier (personal communication)[2], the informants had to select eight sentences to be inserted between the start and the final sentences. They were instructed to attempt to create a coherent text consisting of a total of ten sentences. Participants were allowed to introduce slight modifications to the pre-set sentences so as to ensure a better fit in relation to their text, but they were not permitted to change the actual content. Time on task was set at 35 minutes.

In this paper, the results for five of the informants have been picked out in order to illustrate the use of the alpha-omega task. Four of the informants were school students – two seventh graders, and two tenth graders; the other was a first-year university student of English. Selection was based on their results for a reading test in Danish. Of the four school students, one in each grade had obtained a low reading score, and one a high score; the university student had achieved a high score. From now on, they will be designated respectively as: Grade 7L, Grade 10L, Grade 7H, Grade 10H and University.

Writing skills

How might we characterise these five informants as regards their writing processes? To answer this question, the verbal protocols for the essays were investigated using the coding scheme developed by Cumming (1989). In this procedure, the episodes of the protocols in which informants verbalise their thinking are analysed with respect to two main features: (1) attention given to aspects of writing and (2) problem solving. 'Aspects of writing' comprises attention to *language, idea, discourse organisation, intentions* and *procedure* (the last mentioned would cover statements such as 'I am going to write a fair copy now'). The coding scheme for 'problem solving' covers the following: *knowledge telling* (without any problem solving); *problem identification* (problem is merely identified but not addressed further); *problem solved* (problem is identified and immediately solved, but no details are provided as to the nature of the problem, or to the ways of solving it); *heuristic searches* (problem is addressed, for example, by assessing alternatives or evaluating it with respect to a criterion) and *dictionary* (informant solves problem by consulting a dictionary). The latter was an additional category included specifically for the present project.

The category 'heuristic searches' covers processing behaviour associated with writing expertise. Table 1 shows the results for the five informants for this category (percentages calculated in relation to the total number of episodes).

Table 1. Percentages of heuristic searches in the verbal protocols for the essays

	Grade 7 L	Grade 7 H	Grade 10 L	Grade 10 H	University
L1 essay	13.1	15.3	15.8	31.4	21.9
L2 essay	5.1	17.9	15.7	22.1	17.6

As can be seen from Table 1, the Grade 10 H and the University informants seem to stand clearly apart from the remainder, and it would seem safe to claim that these two informants demonstrate high degrees of writing expertise. The table also shows that the extra processing load of having to operate in the L2 might account for the lower percentages for three of the informants in the L2 protocols (Grade 7 L; Grade 10 H & the university student).

For attention to textual organisation in general, a similar grouping of the informants emerges with reference to discourse organisation, as shown in Table 2. It might be assumed that a high level of writing expertise enabled the Grade 10 H and the University informants to devote more attention to the textual organisation of their essays than the other informants. However, Table 2 also reveals a distinction in the group with lower heuristic searches. The Grade 7 L student pays almost no attention to this aspect of writing, whereas the Grade 7 H student devotes much more, surpassing the Grade 10 L student in this aspect of the task.

Table 2. Percentages of attention paid to discourse organisation

	Grade 7 L	Grade 7 H	Grade 10 L	Grade 10 H	University
L1 essay	1.6	9.7	6.5	14.4	13.2
L2 essay	1.0	8.1	6.3	10.2	11.3

Attention to argumentation in the essay protocols

So far we have established that both the Grade 10 H student and the University student have high levels of writing skills. The question now is whether their verbal protocols reveal any attention to argumentation. This would be the expectation, since the manner in which they process when writing should enable them to focus on matters other than mere idea generation, as has already been indicated by their results for discourse organisation. Various aspects of argumentation are indeed introduced by these two participants into from 4 to 5 per cent of all episodes in both languages. However, the other three students (with one exception) mention argumentation in only between 1 and 2 per cent of all episodes. The notable exception is the Grade 7 H student, who in her English essay considers argumentation in 4.5 per cent of episodes, which implies that in producing her English essay, this informant is as much involved with argumentation as is either of the two most proficient students. These are of course small-scale data that furthermore do not reveal anything about the nature of the attention given to argumentation. Let us now, therefore, examine the verbalisations in more detail.

University student
In the essay protocols, this student decides on her own point of view, defines her opponent and the opposing point of view, and then states arguments for and against her own position. In other words, she deals explicitly with all the points listed above, except refutation of counter-arguments. However, an impressionistic examination of her work reveals that, although her protocols do not show any attention to refuting counter-arguments, rebuttals are included in her essays.

Grade 7 L student
This student deals with argumentation in one episode only per language, at the very beginning of his essay work. In the Danish essay, he simply takes up a standpoint. However, in his English essay, the informant takes up a point of view, and then turns his attention to his opponent, only to state the difficulty of persuading somebody else – who this 'somebody else' is, and what their views are, are matters left unmentioned. Again an impressionistic assessment of his essays reveals that he has difficulties addressing the questions posed in the writing prompts, and he ends his Danish essay by writing, 'Det var det hele.' ['That was all.'] This is a form of conclusion generally associated with immature approaches to writing (cf. knowledge telling as defined by Bereiter and Scardamalia 1987).

The other students
These two participants represent extreme ends of a developmental

continuum, with the other informants being intermediate, also in terms of their attention to argumentation. Thus the Grade 10 H student takes up a standpoint, makes a list of arguments for and against, but defines his opponent only in his English protocol. The Grade 10 L student decides on her point of view and identifies pro arguments to support this. Only in her Danish protocol does she indirectly address the role of her opponent when she considers discarding an argument on the grounds that it is one inappropriate to use when writing to a person with whom you disagree. In her Danish essay protocol, the Grade 7 H student chooses her standpoint and then outlines arguments in support of this. She draws in no counter-arguments, neither does she mention – let alone define – her opponent in any of her protocols. Her English protocol reveals that her higher percentage of attention to argumentation derives simply from her great difficulties in drawing up a pro and con list during the initial planning.

Taken all in all, only the University student demonstrates knowledge of extended argumentation in the essay protocol. But can one trust verbal protocols as reliable evidence of informants' knowledge of argumentation? To attempt to answer this question, let us now turn to the results of the alpha-omega task.

The alpha-omega task

We shall first look at the quality of the short alpha-omega texts produced by the informants and then deal with the results of the analyses of the verbal protocols. (The English alpha-omega texts are reproduced in the appendix.)

The alpha-omega texts

As previously mentioned, Coirier and colleagues used the alpha-omega task to categorise their informants as either more or less proficient at argumentation. They did not use verbal protocols, but they judged the ability of informants to argue by assessing the actual texts they produced. For this process, they devised a scoring system that took into account thematisation in addition to argumentative orientation. According to their scoring system, all the texts from our group of informants would be categorised as 'expert' texts. The youngest participants in our study are slightly older than the *oldest* informants in the studies performed by the Coirier et al. research team. So whereas in their case some participants only satisfied the scoring criteria for thematisation, all our informants are well beyond that point. Their scoring system is consequently not sensitive enough to bring out differences between the informants in the present project.

Nonetheless, the texts produced by our informants are very different –

even though such differences fail to be captured by the scoring system. Notably, they vary in regard to argumentative orientation. In some instances what might be termed a 'fifty/fifty solution' was furnished: in the first half of the text, the informants presented four arguments supporting the initial statement, and, in the second half, replied with four arguments in favour of the final statement. Such an approach is what might be expected from those students inclined to present one-sided argumentation; they accept the start and end sentences as two valid claims, and so give equal support to both. Fifty/fifty solutions of this sort are found with the Grade 7 L student for both languages, and in the Grade 10 L student for the L1. The other texts, apart from exhibiting a better balance towards the end sentence, also indicate the shift from pro-alpha to pro-omega very clearly. The University student and the Grade 10 H student both use two conjunctions to indicate the shift from support for the start statement to the end statement. Only the word 'but' signals the same radical shift in argument (in L1 and L2) for the Grade 7 L and Grade 10 L students. The Grade 7 H student is truly remarkable in all respects. In addition to using two conjunctions to mark the above-mentioned shift in both languages, she is unique in using a counter-argument to the end sentence in the last part of her L2 text; consequently she alone produces a text that has the structure presented in Figure 1 above.

To judge from the alpha-omega texts only, the Grade 7 L and the Grade 10 L students seem to lag behind the others in the ability to write argumentative texts. Let us now turn to the informants' verbalisations produced while solving the alpha-omega task.

The alpha-omega protocols
The analysis of the verbal protocols for this task was carried out using essentially the same categories that had been employed for analysing the essay protocols. Only slight modifications needed to be introduced, notably subcategories to the category *attention to discourse organisation*.

It has often previously been stated that, compared to the writing of an essay, the alpha-omega task is a task that places relatively few demands on the learners' processing capacity. The considerable reduction in the processing load is borne out by the percentages for *attention to discourse organisation*, as shown in Table 3.

Table 3. Percentages of attention to discourse organisation

	Grade 7 L	Grade 7 H	Grade 10 L	Grade 10 H	University
L1 AO task	19.5 (17.1)	31.5 (19.2)	29.5 (19.2)	57.4 (13.9)	44.1 (30.1)
L2 AO task	17.1 (17.1)	31.0 (5.6)	47.9 (35.3)	68.1 (10.4)	45.1 (23.3)

This table shows that there is a marked increase in *attention to discourse organisation* in alpha-omega as compared with the essays (see Table 2). This is not of course very surprising since in essence what the informants have to cope with in this task is putting the sentences together to form a text. However, for the analysis of the verbal protocols of the alpha-omega task, this category takes in a number of subcategories, one of which covers episodes in which the informants announce their choice of a given sentence. In Table 3, the percentages in brackets cover the results for this category. This means that all the attention of the Grade 7 L student is riveted on choosing sentences in his L2 protocol, while for the other students the percentages of this sub-category represent various proportions of their attention to discourse organisation. Other sub-categories indicate the students' concern with argumentation, with themes and sub-themes. It is fairly clear that those students who produced a good alpha-omega text also paid attention to the other matters captured by the sub-categories, namely argumentation, theme and sub-theme.[3]

We find interesting differences in attention to argumentation in these protocols taking the results of this task vis-à-vis those for the essays. Table 4 gives the degrees of attention to argumentation for both writing tasks.

Table 4. Percentages of attention to argumentation in the verbal protocols for the essays and the alpha-omega task

	Grade 7 L	Grade 7 H	Grade 10 L	Grade 10 H	University
L1 essay	1.6	1.7	1.8	4.5	3.9
L2 essay	1.0	4.5	1.8	4.6	5.1
L1 AO task	2.4	6.8	6.4	21.3	5.9
L2 AO task	0	12.7	5.0	26.4	8.3

These figures show that the level of attention to argumentation is very similar for the two tasks not only for the Grade 7 L student but also for the University student. We can conclude that the Grade 7 L informant has not benefited from the reduced processing load of the alpha-omega task. It is therefore a feasible assumption that this student has neither the writing skills nor the knowledge of argumentation required for the task.

The other three students definitely show an increase in attention to argumentation in the alpha-omega task – the Grade 10 H student demonstrating this to an extreme extent. Let us now investigate exactly what these percentages represent. The high percentages for the Grade 10 H student are obtained because in both languages he starts by classifying all the sentences on the basis of whether or not they are arguments for or against either the start or the end sentence. He then actually constructs a small diagram for counting how many sentences fall into each type, clearly feeling this task to be one centred around argument. In addition to this, he also attends to global planning of the short text, which can be seen in the extract from his L2 protocol below.[4] (Translations into English, preserving the disconnected language typical of verbal protocols, have been provided throughout.)

Original
– og så tager jeg to plus-sætninger.. til eller… ja to øhm plus-sætninger om bilen så to minus-sætninger om bilen… så øøh og så fire plus-sætninger om toget… så.. det vil f.eks. komme til at se sådan her ud.. – <the car is practical because.. the car is practical>

Translation
– and then I'll take two plus sentences …. for or …. yes two um plus sentences for the car then two minus sentences for the car … then um and then four plus sentences for the train … then .. that it will sound like this – <the car is practical because.. the car is practical>
(The student then starts reading the sentences in the order just indicated.)

This extract above shows that the student is planning for an appropriate balance between arguments in favour of both alpha and omega. As can be seen in the extract below, from her Danish protocol, the Grade 10 L student also takes account of global planning, but compared to the example above, her planning is qualitatively very different. She has decided on a fifty/fifty solution and keeps to this, as can be seen from her final text.

Original
– otte otteren skal også med otte det vil sige jeg tager fire for lejlighed og så tager jeg fire for øh for øh for at bo hjemme –

Translation
– eight number eight should also be included eight in other words I'll take four for the flat and then I'll take four for um for um for living at home –

So for these two students, the striking increase in attention to argumentation for the Grade 10 H student coincides with high quality of argumentation, and similarly the less marked increase for the Grade 10 L student coincides with low quality of argumentation.

Turning to the Grade 7 H student, we find that she operates very much in the same way as the older students. This also holds true for global planning, as is indicated in the extracts below, all taken from her English protocol. In the first of these, she is making a rough plan:

Original
<it is nice to live in a village> – ja .. det er det jo [laughs] øhm så skal jeg m finde nogle gode ting ved en landsby så til sidst så vil jeg bruge nogen af dem der som er ikke så gode om en landsby og så vil jeg så bruge nogle af dem som er ret gode om en by og så kan jeg så slutte med – <that is why it is better to live in a city>

Translation
<it is nice to live in a village> – yes .. that is that is of course [laughs] um then I have to find some good things about a village then at the end I'll use some of those that are not so good about a village and then I'll then use some of those that are rather good about a city and then I'll finish with – <that is why it is better to live in a city>

In the second extract, she considers how many of the different kinds of arguments to put in her text and finally decides that she needs even more sentences in favour of omega vis-à-vis alpha.

Original
traffic is not very busy in a village – hovsa ….. nå ja [clears throat] det {er jo} også en god ting og så vil jeg finde noget hvor jeg for eksempel kan sige *and* bla bla bla bla øhm og så bagefter så vil jeg så sige skal lige se hvor mange {er så} tre { } delt op fire tror jeg skal have *to* gode grunde til hvorfor det er godt a bo i en øhm en landsby *to* dårlige grunde til hvorfor det ikke er særlig godt og to gode grunde til at det er .. øhm .. det er bedre at bo en by {og det vil sige} to gode to knap så gode to gooo nej det passer ikke jeg tror jeg tager så tager jeg tre gode om at bo i en landsby nej to gode og to dårlige så tager jeg .. øhm .. fire der er bedre [rustles paper] {om en} ej tre gode om en landsby tager jeg og så tager jeg to dårlige og så tager jeg så tre dårlige nej men det skal jo egentlig det skal jo være noget med at der er flere gode flere der er der er flere gode grunde til altså der er der er *endnu* flere gode grunde til at bo i en by og derfor så skal jeg have

flere så derfor siger jeg tager .. tager to då to gode grunde til at bo i en landsby og så tager jeg så tre dårlige grunde til at bo i en landsby og så tager jeg tre gode grunde til at bo i en by så skal jeg finde på en til god om en landsby lige kigger lige engang .. øhm ..and –

Translation
traffic is not very busy in a village – hey ...... well yes [clears throat] it {is of course} also a good thing and then I'll find something where I can say for instance *and* bla bla bla bla um and then after that then I'll then say I need to see how many {it's then} three {   } divided four I think I need to have *two* good reasons as to why it is good to live in a um a village *two* bad reasons as to why it isn't very all that good and two good reasons for it being .. um .. it being better to live a city {that is} two not so good two goo- no that does not fit I think I'll take then I'll take three good about living in a village no two good and two bad then I'll take .. um .. four that's better [rustles paper] {about a} no three good ones about a village I'll take that and then I'll take two bad ones and then I'll take then three bad ones no but in fact it has to be something like that there need to be more good more that are there need to be more good reasons for it okay there need there need to be *even* more good reasons for living in a city and therefore then I need more so therefore I say I take .. take two ba- two good reasons for living in a village and then I'll take then three bad reasons for living in a village and then I'll take three good reasons for living in a city then I need to find one more good about a village let me just have a look .. um ..and –

A third extract from her protocol is presented below, although it is not an episode that has been coded as demonstrating attention to argumentation, but rather as attention to language, as is shown by the use of the connecting phrase *even though*. The episode can be interpreted as indicating that the student is here verbalising her considerations in deciding to employ a counter-argument to omega, and clearly signalling it as such.

Original
– ja [clears throat] øh .. even though kunne jeg måske godt bruge noget med .. even though there is .. very much traffic {er der noget ved at sige det} … øhm ja det tror jeg {jeg vil finde} even though .. even though .. hvor {det var} der var noget med traffic i hvert fald … øh even though – <the traffic is very busy in a city>

Translation
– yes [clears throat] um .. 'even though' I might be able to use something with that .. even though there is .. very much traffic {do I gain anything by saying this} ... um yes I think so {I'll find} even though .. even though .. where {it was} it was something to do with traffic at any rate ... um even though – <the traffic is very busy in a city>

For this student, one could assume that although she possesses knowledge, or awareness, of argumentation, her writing process is not yet sufficiently developed for her to take note of the many constraints involved in producing an argumentative text for an essay.

Conclusion

We have examined the writing processes of five learners from three different educational levels pertaining to two very dissimilar writing tasks. *The essay task*, which comes closest to an actual writing situation, helped us identify the degree of writing expertise possessed by the five informants. The University student managed to take account of all save one of the constraints of argumentative writing in her verbal protocols for the essays; no other participant achieved this. It was apparent that the Grade 7 L student demonstrated neither the writing skills nor the knowledge needed for this kind of text production. Of the three other students, one – the Grade 10 H student – demonstrated considerable strength in writing skills, but it was difficult to judge from his verbalisation whether or not he had the knowledge needed for argumentative text production. The other two lagged behind both in writing skills and attention to argumentation. In both these cases, it was difficult to ascertain their level of knowledge of argumentation on the basis of the relatively few sporadic comments in their protocols.

When the performance of these students on *the alpha-omega task* is also taken into account, a number of the problems mentioned here were partly solved. For instance, the Grade 7 L student did not reveal any insights as regards argumentation, thus confirming the impression formed on the basis of his essay task. The alpha-omega task also confirmed the assessment made of the Grade 10 L student from her performance on the essay task. On the other hand, the Grade 7 H student clearly demonstrated awareness of argumentation once the processing load of essay writing had been reduced for her. In her case, the alpha-omega task allows us to conclude with some certainty that her problem with writing an argumentative text should be attributed to lack of writing skills rather than to lack of knowledge of argumentation. Finally, the Grade 10 H student showed an almost extreme degree of attention to argumentation in the protocols for this task, thus correcting the apparently false assumptions that the essay protocols had produced. This result runs counter to our initial claim that knowledge of argumentation is likely to be revealed in essay protocols, provided that the informant has high levels of writing skills. There are of course many factors that might account for this, such as the informant's assessment of the four constraints mentioned earlier, namely the preconditions for argumentation to occur in the first place. The data available in this project does not lend itself to addressing these issues directly. There is, however, one important source of data that has been referred to so far only in an unsystematic way, namely the actual essays. Proper analysis of the argumentative structure of the students' essays is definitely an avenue that we intend to go down within this project.

Notes

[1] The authors gratefully acknowledge financial support from the Danish National Research Council for the Humanities (Statens Humanistiske Forskningsråd) in the form of a three year research grant which has made this study possible. The authors also wish to thank Alister Cumming for his generous advice concerning the planning of the project. Any errors or shortcomings remain, of course, entirely the authors' responsibility.

[2] The authors wish to express their gratitude for the time spent by Jerry Andriessen and Pierre Coirier in advising us on the use of the alpha-omega task. Any shortcomings in interpretation and use of the task remain, of course, entirely the authors' responsibility.

[3] Coirier et al. (1999: 23) are cautious in claiming that the results for the alpha-omega task also apply in actual writing situations. From the results of the protocol analyses of the essay, and alpha-omega task for the few students presented here, it would seem likely that the alpha-omega task does indeed tap into writing ability in general.

[4] The coding system for the transcriptions of protocols is as follows:

* *	= actual writing sequences
< >	= reading aloud of text already produced, or of the writing prompt
– –	= comments/verbalisation of thinking
[ ]	= indicates coughing, laughing, sighing etc.
.. ..	= rough indications of length of pauses
{ }	= inaudible, or partly inaudible, portions of protocol (if partly audible, text represents transcriber's best guess; if totally inaudible, blank space provides rough indication of length)

References

Andriessen, J., Coirier, P., Roos, L., Passerault, J-M. and Bert-Erboul, A. (1996) 'Thematic and Structural Planning in Constrained Argumentative Text Production', in G. Rijlaarsdam, H. van den Bergh and M. Couzijn (eds.), *Theories, Models and Methodology in Writing Research*, 237-251, Amsterdam University Press: Amsterdam.

Bereiter, C. and Scardamalia, M. (1987) *The Psychology of Written Composition*, Lawrence Erlbaum: Hillsdale, NJ.

Coirier, P., Andriessen, J. and Chanquoy, L. (1999) 'From Planning to Translating: the Specificity of Argumentative Writing', in J. Andriessen and P. Coirier (eds.), *Foundations of Argumentative Text Processing*, 1-28, Amsterdam University Press: Amsterdam.

Cumming, A. (1989) 'Writing Expertise and Second-Language Proficiency', *Language Learning* **39**, 1, 81-141.

Cumming, A. (1990) 'Metalinguistic and Ideational Thinking in Second Language Composing', *Written Communication* **7**, 4, 482-511.

Ericsson, K. A. and Simon, H.A. (1993) *Protocol Analysis. Verbal Reports as Data*, MIT Press: Cambridge, MA.

Freedman, A. and Pringle, I. (1989) 'Contexts for Developing Argument', in R. Andrews (ed.), *Narrative and Argument*, 73-84, Open University Press: Milton Keynes. Philadelphia.

Jourdenais, R. (2001) 'Cognition, Instruction and Protocol Analysis', in P. Robinson (ed.), *Cognition and Second Language Instruction*, 354-375, Cambridge University Press: Cambridge.

Kuhn, D. (1991) *The Skills of Argument*, Cambridge University Press: Cambridge.

Roca de Larios, J., Marín, J. and Murphy, L. (2001) 'A Temporal Analysis of Formulation Processes in L1 and L2 Writing', *Language Learning*, **51**, 497-538.

Smagorinsky, P. (1994) 'Think-Aloud Protocol Analysis: Beyond the Black Box', in P. Smagorinsky (ed.), *Speaking about Writing. Reflections on Research Methodology*, 3-19, SAGE Publications: Thousand Oaks, London, New Delhi.

Whalen, K. and Ménard, N. (1995) 'L1 and L2 Writers' Strategic and Linguistic Knowledge: a Model of Multiple-Level Discourse Processing', *Language Learning* **45**, 381- 418.

Appendix

The following are the actual English alpha-omega texts produced by the five students (spelling and punctuation unchanged).

University high

It is nice to live in a village. It is nice and quiet, and life is less hectic than in the city. But there is nothing much to do in a village, and you have to drive a long way to get anywhere. However, there is always something to do in a city, there are many different and exciting people and many places are within reach: a swimming-pool, a theatre, a cinema: they are all there. That is why it is better to live in a city.

Grade 10 H

The car is practical. In a car you can go anywhere you like at any time, and the car is practical when you are going on holiday far away. However, if your car breaks down you have to wait for help to come. In a car it can be difficult to find somewhere to park, but you do not have to find a parking space when you go by train. Sometimes the car will not start so, in wintertime the train is safer than the car, plus you don't have to remove ice/snow from the windows of your car when you go by train. That is why the train is more practical than the car.

Grade 10 L

It is nice to live in a village. In a village it is nice and quiet. A village is very sociable, you know almost everyone. There is less air pollution in a village. But, when you live in a village, you have to drive a long way to get anywhere. A swimming-pool, a theatre, a cinema: they are all there in the city. In a city the shops are nearby, so you can walk to them. There is nothing much to do in a village. And in a city there are many different and exciting people. That is why it is better to live in a city.

Grade 7 H

It is nice to live in a village. The traffic is not very Busy in a village and in a village it is nice and quiet. But when you live in a village, you have to drive a long way to get anywhere And there is not much to do in a village. There is always something to do in a city. Even though the traffic is very Busy in a city, It is nice because many places are within reach, Like a swimming Pool, a theatre, a cinema: they are all there in the city. That is why it is better to live in a city.

Grade 7 L

The train is practical. Becuse if your car breaks down you have to waite fore help to come. And the train is practical becuse you dont have to drive yourself. On the train you can read or look out of the window and traffic jams is irritating. But when you go by train you cannot leave whenever you want. And you can take a lot of luggage whit your car The car is more practic becuse you can go anyway you like at any time And the car can stop outside your door That is why the car is more practical that the train.

METAPHORICAL COMPETENCE AND THE L2 LEARNER

Anna Cieślicka and David Singleton

ABSTRACT

This article attempts to show how theoretical research into metaphorical language can be employed to shed light on the nature of L2 learning and how implications stemming from theoretical findings may find application in the L2 classroom. The article starts with a definition of metaphorical competence and with some comments on the changing view of metaphor in language studies. It then focuses on a particular area of metaphor research that has evoked much controversy among metaphor scholars, namely, the conceptual metaphor view of figurative language. The final part of the article is devoted to a review of L2 studies which have drawn on the conceptual metaphor research findings and ends with some reflections on the pedagogical applicability of such findings.

Introduction

In this article we review a particular area of research relating to metaphorical competence and explore its possible implications for L2 lexical learning in the classroom. According to Levorato, native language metaphorical or figurative competence subsumes such skills as:

> the ability to break down an idiom into its component parts and to make semantic inferences about these; the ability to comprehend idiomatic expressions even when they have been subjected to lexical substitution or syntactic and lexical variations; and the ability to generate new idioms by means of syntactic and lexical variations on existing idioms.
>
> (Levorato 1993: 122).

Danesi (1992) claims that lack of metaphorical competence is a major reason why L2 learners fail to become native-like and that metaphorical competence is usually inadequate in classroom L2 learners even after years of learning (cf. also e.g. Alexander 1987; Irujo 1993; Kecskes and Papp 2000; Kovesces and Szabó 1996; Lattey 1986; Low 1988; Moon 1997; Zughoul 1991). Danesi (1992) further argues that metaphorical competence should be the subject of instruction and urges educators to develop instructional techniques to this end. An obvious source of insights for the elaboration of such techniques is research into metaphorical processing.

We begin with a few general observations on the deployment of metaphor in early and everyday L1 use; we go on to focus on a specific strand of metaphor research, the conceptual metaphor perspective; finally we give an account of some L2 studies which have drawn on conceptual metaphor research findings, including some which appear to have implications for teaching.

Changing views of metaphor

There was a time when metaphor was regarded as 'a sort of happy extra trick with language' (Richards 1936: 90) – or even an abuse of language (Hobbes 1651: Part 1, Chapter 4). Even today there is a widespread view that metaphor is primarily associated with literary, scientific or philosophical discourse. In fact, however, metaphor is everywhere in language, and from the earliest stages. Singleton (1999: 71), citing Elliot (1981) notes that children's semantic over-extensions in their early deployment of words can be attributed to the operation of a capacity for metaphorical extension. For example, the child who sees a centipede for the first time and calls it a *comb* (Clark 1993: 34) seems to be exhibiting just such a capacity (cf. Winner 1997). The omnipresence of metaphor is also exemplified by the constantly changing lexicon of teenage slang, additions to which are overwhelmingly figurative in nature (cf. e.g. Singleton and Ryan forthcoming, Chapter 3).

One view of metaphor, indeed, is that it lies at the very heart of our coming to grips with the world. This is the position of Lakoff and others (Lakoff 1987, 1990; 1993; Lakoff and Johnson 1980; Lakoff and Turner 1989), who have suggested that metaphor is as much a matter of thought as it is of language. It is the central tenet of the conceptual metaphor view of figurative language, to which we now turn.

The conceptual metaphor view of figurative language

The theory and studies supporting it
Gibbs (1992, 1994, 1996, 1998, 2001) argues that most linguistic metaphors reflect underlying metaphorical correspondences which constitute part of the human conceptual system. He claims that metaphorical expressions are understood effortlessly and without being perceived as deviant or anomalous; and that this results from the fact that most figurative expressions are instantiations of pre-existing conceptual metaphorical mappings between conceptual domains. Thus, he suggests that the expression *Our marriage is a rollercoaster ride* is understood via the underlying conceptual metaphor LOVE

IS A JOURNEY (Gibbs 1994) and that the concept of love can also be understood through other metaphors – including LOVE IS INSANITY, LOVE IS A VALUABLE COMMODITY, LOVE IS A HIDDEN OBJECT (cf. Kovecses 1986).

Gibbs and O'Brien (1990) examined mental images of idiomatic phrases referring to anger (*blow your stack*, etc.), exerting control (*crack the whip*, etc.), insanity (*lose your marbles*, etc.), and revelation (*spill the beans*, etc.). It transpired that their participants' mental images for different idioms belonging to the same figurative group were highly consistent, which Gibbs and O'Brien (1990) took to reflect the constraining influence of underlying metaphorical knowledge. Thus, mental images for the anger idioms included some force causing a container to release pressure in a violent way. These images, according to the authors, reflect the conceptual metaphor ANGER IS HEATED FLUID IN A CONTAINER (cf. also Gibbs 1994). In another study, Nayak and Gibbs (1990) constructed contexts such as a story involving Mary waiting for Bob, who had failed to come home early to help her prepare for a dinner party, which depicted Mary's growing anger in terms of increasing pressure and heat – through the use of such phrases as *she was getting hotter* and *the pressure was really building up*. The last, unfinished line of the story *When Bob strolled in at ten minutes to five whistling and smiling, Mary…*, was followed by two idiomatic expressions, *blew her top*, and *bit his head off* only the former of which reflected the same conceptual metaphor as that depicted in the story. Participants' ratings of the appropriateness of each idiomatic ending showed that they were sensitive to the congruence between the conceptual metaphor primed by contexts and that underlying the idioms.

Gibbs (1992) also looked at mental images associated with non-idiomatic metaphorical expressions. Again, striking inter-participant similarities emerged. For example, for the phrase *Some marriages are iceboxes*, 84% of his participants reported an image of a large freezer containing a frozen couple. Most agreed that the couple had not entered the freezer willingly, that they were unhappy to be there, that they were dissatisfied with each other, and that getting out of the freezer was difficult. For Gibbs, such consistency evidences the constraining presence of the conceptual metaphor RELATIONSHIPS ARE CONTAINERS. He found that consistency in mental images did not hold for literal phrases, which he interprets as indicating that, unlike metaphorical expressions, literal expressions are not motivated by conceptual metaphors. In subsequent research, Gibbs and Beitel (1995) and Gibbs, Strom and Spivey-Knowlton (1997) asked participants to describe their mental images for proverbs. Again, the mental images were strikingly consistent, which Gibbs again explains by reference to the constraining influence of conceptual metaphors.

Conceptual metaphors are in addition claimed to facilitate discourse comprehension. Research by Allbritton, McKoon and Gerrig (1995) suggests that metaphor-based schemas form connections between elements within a text. Participants read brief passages exhibiting schemas based on conceptual metaphors and containing sentences consistent with these conceptual metaphors. For example, a passage based on the conceptual metaphor CRIME IS A DISEASE described increasing crime statistics and extra police patrols unsuccessfully struggling with a city's crime epidemic. The last sentence of the text, *Public officials desperately looked for a cure*, was clearly related to the earlier occurring *The city's epidemic was raging out of control*, both instantiating the CRIME IS A DISEASE schema. On the other hand, in a changed-context condition, the context preceding the sentence *Public officials desperately looked for a cure* was modified so as to make it refer to a virulent strain of pneumonia, thus no longer instantiating the metaphor CRIME IS A DISEASE. After reading the passages, participants were given a cued-recognition test for words or sentences they had read. It was found that words and sentences preceded by a prime related to the same metaphor-based schema as the test item were recognized faster than those preceded by primes instantiating a different schema. Thus, the sentence *Public officials desperately looked for a cure* was recognized faster when preceded by the sentence *The city's crime epidemic was raging out of control* only when the two sentences instantiated the same schema. Allbritton et al. see these results as supporting the claim that metaphor-based schemas play a role in discourse comprehension, helping to connect pieces of information in a text representation.

Metaphorical knowledge has also been shown to influence the use and understanding of euphemisms. Pfaff, Gibbs, and Johnson (1997) investigated the appropriateness of euphemistic phrases in stories with varying metaphorical contexts. Participants read stories differing in terms of metaphorical context and euphemistic final phrases. Participants had to rate the final phrase according to its fit with the preceding context. For example, the story: *Dirk is a real wolf. He prowls the singles bars looking for unsuspecting young women to proposition. One night he saw a particularly tasty-looking morsel in a miniskirt and said to his friend*, was designed to prime the conceptual metaphor SEXUAL DESIRE IS A HUNTING ANIMAL. Following this story, participants saw either the metaphor-consistent story-final sentence *I'm ready to pounce*, or a conceptual metaphor-inconsistent sentence: *She's turning my crank*. The results supported Pfaff et al.'s prediction that euphemistic final sentences would be rated as more appropriate and easier to process when they were conceptually consistent with the preceding context, which they interpret as supporting their view that metaphorical conceptualizations influence use and understanding of different kinds of euphemism.

Challenges to the conceptual metaphor view
Other studies have failed to demonstrate the presence of conceptual metaphors in the interpretation of figurative language. McGlone (1996) asked participants to paraphrase metaphors purportedly instantiating conceptual metaphors. Responses were quite divergent, less than ¼ being construable as motivated by underlying conceptual metaphors. Similar results were obtained for a task in which participants were asked to provide paraphrases of metaphors. McGlone concludes that conceptual metaphors are not actively involved in constructing interpretations of metaphoric expressions. Glucksberg (1995) also takes issue with Gibbs's view, suggesting that rather than a static, pre-stored mapping being retrieved from long term memory, the necessary schema is generated when the figurative expression is first encountered; and that the generated schema is used to project on to the metaphor topic or target domain all the relevant attributes of the vehicle, or source domain. The relevant mappings can, according to Glucksberg, be retained and accessed on subsequent occasions. This theoretical approach has been developed over the last two decades by Glucksberg and his colleagues under the name of the *class inclusion, attributive categorization,* or *interactive property attribution model* (Camac and Glucksberg 1984; Glucksberg 1991, 1995, 2001, Glucksberg, Gildea, and Bookin 1982; Glucksberg and Keysar 1990; Glucksberg, Keysar, and McGlone 1992; Glucksberg, McGlone, and Manfredi 1997; Glucksberg, Newsome, and Goldvarg 2001). More recently, Glucksberg (2001) has referred to his model as the *dual-reference attribution model*. On this proposal, language users assign the topic of the metaphor to a diagnostic, ad hoc category which is inferred from the expression and which the vehicle concept exemplifies. In such assertions, the metaphor vehicle refers to that category and can actually be seen as a prototypical exemplar of that category. For instance, in the metaphor *My job is a jail*, the topic *my job* cannot plausibly belong to the category of *buildings* labelled by the vehicle *jail*. Therefore, rather than considering this category as the basis for interpreting the metaphorical expression, the reader or listener infers a category of entities that the vehicle refers to (e.g. the set of situations that are unpleasant, confining, punishing, and unrewarding). This category might not have a conventional name of its own, but when it is employed to characterize the topic, it starts functioning as an attributive category, by

providing features that can be subsequently attributed to the topic (unpleasant, unrewarding, confining, etc.) (Glucksberg and Keysar 1990).

Glucksberg and Keysar further suggest that the metaphor vehicle, which is a prototypical member of this unconventional category inferred in the course of metaphor interpretation, can actually lend its name to the category itself. With repeated use, the attributive category exemplified by the metaphor vehicle may gradually become part of a term's conventional meaning, in which case a previously nonlexicalized category becomes lexicalized, in that it receives a name. An example of a new category that received its name from one of its prototypical members is *Vietnam*, which refers to disastrous military interventions (Glucksberg, 2001). Thus, in the statement *Cambodia has become Vietnam's Vietnam*, the term *Vietnam* performs two different functions. Whereas in the first occurrence it refers to the country itself, in the second it refers figuratively to disastrous military interventions that the Vietnam war symbolizes. The fact that in metaphor comprehension a vehicle term can have both concrete and abstract referents has been labelled *dual reference* by Glucksberg (2001). Vehicles, thus, on Glucksberg et al.'s (1990) view, provide a set of general characteristics which are then attributed to and further specified by metaphor topics.

Glucksberg, Keysar and McGlone (1992) asked college students to provide paraphrases of three metaphors suggested by Gibbs (1992) to be motivated by the LOVE IS A JOURNEY conceptual metaphor, namely: *Our love is a bumpy roller coaster ride, Our love is a voyage to the bottom of the sea,* and *Our love is a dusty road travelled*. Gibbs's view predicts that paraphrases of such expressions should be relatively consistent. In contrast, Glucksberg's interactive property attribution view of metaphor comprehension claims that interpreting these metaphors entails assigning the metaphor topic to the attributive-diagnostic category typified by the metaphor vehicle, and that, since the metaphor vehicles may typify different things for different people, the resulting interpretations of these metaphorical expressions should vary. What Glucksberg *et al.* found was that interpretations were not only divergent; they also failed to make reference to any journey-related properties. Glucksberg *et al.* interpret their results as corroborating the position that people do not automatically access conventional metaphorical mappings when interpreting metaphorical expressions. Glucksberg and McGlone (1999) suggest that in situations requiring conscious and deliberate analysis people may recognize the conventional metaphorical mappings postulated as underlying metaphorical expressions, but that in the routine comprehension of metaphorical language conceptual analogies between source and target domains are not routinely accessed. Glucksberg (2001) goes on to critique the claim that knowledge of abstract concepts is subsumed by knowledge of concrete concepts, which, he suggests, is called into question by the capacity to distinguish between the literal and the metaphorical. He further comments that the conceptual metaphor view fails to provide an account of how a language user can identify the particular conceptual metaphor relevant to understanding a given figurative expression.

Murphy (1996, 1997) also challenges the conceptual metaphor view of figurative language comprehension, suggesting that data cited as evidence for conceptual metaphor representations can often be accounted for by structural similarity between domains. On this view, metaphors arise out of the similarity of conceptual structures – e.g. argument and war –, rather than out of the essentially metaphoric structure of human cognition or the metaphoric nature of the concepts themselves. Murphy (1996) proposes that, 'structural similarity permits people to construct understandable verbal metaphors' and that 'those that are most interesting or revealing 'stick' and may become conventional' (p. 179). Murphy (1997) also argues that unless a model of metaphoric thought addresses the questions of what metaphoric concepts are, how they are structured, accessed and coordinated, and how people choose among different possible metaphors in a given situation, it remains incomplete. These criticisms are rebutted by Gibbs (1996, 1999) but remain a major challenge for the conceptual metaphor position.

Conceptual metaphors and L2 learning

Turning now to L2-oriented metaphor research, it has dealt with various aspects of metaphorical language processing, such as understanding idioms, metaphors, and various multi-word units (e.g. phrasal verbs) the acquisition of which constitutes an essential component of L2 metaphorical competence. Bortfeld (2002) asked native and non-native English speakers to form mental images of familiar English idioms. Even when explicitly instructed to construct their images on the basis of the idioms' literal meanings, both groups of participants reported images which reflected a combination of the idioms' literal and figurative senses. For example, the mental image created by one participant in reaction to the idiom 'Go off your rocker' included a person getting off their rocking chair to get some food, whereas another image included a scene in which a crazy woman kept rocking in her rocking chair until she lost her grip on the chair and fell over. This finding suggests, according to Bortfeld, that non-native speakers, like native speakers, map idioms' surface forms to underlying conceptual metaphors. In another experiment, Bortfeld asked non-natives to create mental images of unfamiliar English idioms before and after they were told what the idioms meant. The images created before and after participants were familiarized with the idioms did not significantly differ, which seems to suggest that imagery for idioms is unaffected by explicit knowledge of their figurative meanings. For Bortfeld this constitutes evidence for the notion that L2 learners find L2 idioms conceptually analysable. Comparison of the images reported by non-native speakers to those reported by native speakers revealed marked similarities, which Bortfeld takes to indicate that specific conceptual structures underlie the meaning of idiomatic phrases and that this should be exploited in L2 instruction.

Cieślicka (2002) examined metaphors about teaching and learning elicited from fluent Polish students of English. In one task the participants were asked to provide metaphorical completions of a sentence stem: 'Teaching is..., because....', 'Learning is..., because....'. The methodology was replicated from a study conducted among English university students in Great Britain by Cortazzi and Jin (1999). The data obtained from this original study served as the basis for comparing metaphors elicited from Polish-English bilingual speakers with the metaphors produced by native speakers of English. The results showed consistency in the conceptual metaphors employed by L2 learners and native speakers of English. Thus, the prevailing responses elicited from the Polish students of English could be categorized as instantiating the following metaphors: TEACHING IS A JOURNEY (e.g. the response 'guiding somebody through a forest'), TEACHING IS FOOD/DRINKING/COOKING (e.g. 'being a chef in an experimental kitchen'), TEACHING IS PLANT GROWTH/CULTIVATION (e.g. 'planting seeds'), TEACHING IS A SKILL (e.g. 'performing a difficult medical operation'), TEACHING IS AN OCCUPATION (e.g. 'being a doctor'), TEACHING IS ENTERTAINMENT (e.g. 'actor's performance'), and TEACHING IS CONSTRUCTION/PART OF A BUILDING (e.g. 'building a house'). Essentially identical metaphors were identified as predominant in Cortazzi and Jinn's (1999) study. This may testify to the universality of conceptual metaphors of teaching and/or imply similar cultural orientations to teaching among Polish and English students participating in the study. Cieślicka also examined the responses of fluent Polish learners of English to questions concerning their own language learning or teaching experience. Participants were not explicitly instructed to provide metaphors, but it was speculated that their accounts might still be characterized by the occurrence of unelicited, spontaneous metaphors, which would constitute strong evidence of a role for conceptual metaphors in L2 figurative competence. However, in this latter case, the number of metaphorical phrases was very small and the range of metaphors much less varied than that obtained in the metaphor elicitation task.

In another study Cieślicka (2003) investigated the knowledge base employed by bilingual language users when interpreting metaphorical expressions in their L2. The experiment required Polish participants to paraphrase, both literally and figuratively, a variety of metaphorical expressions in their L2 (English), each of which instantiated conceptual metaphors identified in the conceptual metaphor literature (Lakoff and Johnson 1980). The participants were also instructed to rate the comprehensibility of each metaphorical sentence and to create novel metaphorical sentences that would express the same idea as the original metaphor. Whereas all of the metaphors appeared to be easily comprehensible, the vast majority of paraphrases (82%) contained no conceptual metaphor references. By way of example, when paraphrasing the metaphor *Dr. Moreland's lecture was a 3-course meal for the mind*, which is supposedly motivated by the conceptual metaphor IDEAS ARE FOOD, the majority of participants failed to include any references to the food domain in their paraphrases, which is what would be expected if understanding and processing metaphorical expressions did indeed entail the obligatory activation of their underlying conceptual metaphorical mappings, in line with the conceptual metaphor view. Some paraphrases could be viewed as being constructed along the lines suggested by Glucksberg's attributive categorization view, which claims that, in the course of interpreting a metaphor, the language user constructs an ad hoc category which the vehicle concept exemplifies and to which the target concept might plausibly belong (see earlier discussion). Thus, when paraphrasing the metaphor *Our marriage was a rollercoaster ride*, many participants interpreted this phrase in terms of the category exemplified by the metaphor vehicle *rollercoaster ride*. Since a rollercoaster ride can be seen as representative of experiences which are thrilling, exciting, fun, and crazy, many participants referred to exactly such characteristics when explaining the meaning of the metaphor (e.g. *Our marriage was extremely exciting, full of adrenaline surges; we never got bored, there was always something happening*). However, there remained numerous paraphrases which could not be explained by reference to either the conceptual metaphor or the attributive categorization view. This was particularly true of metaphors containing ambiguous vehicles, which did not unequivocally suggest a category under which the metaphor topic might be subsumed. One such example was the metaphor stimulus *Her mind is a shoebox*, conceptually motivated by the metaphor MIND IS A CONTAINER. The paraphrases provided in response to this metaphor not only overwhelmingly failed to include any reference to the source domain of containers, but they also failed to comply with the attributive categorization view, in that they included such varying accounts as *She has the capacity of great retention of facts* on the one hand and *She is narrow-minded* on the other.

Similar results were obtained from a metaphor generation task, in which participants created their own metaphors. The majority of the generated metaphors (65%) failed to exhibit any correspondence to the underlying conceptual metaphor source domain. Instead, a number of metaphorical productions preserved the stereotypical properties of the original vehicle concept, consistent with the attributive categorization view of metaphor processing. Thus, metaphors generated in response to the Dr. Moreland expression, quoted earlier, included in the chracteristics of the vehicle (*the three-course meal*) that could be attributed to the topic *lecture*, such as for example, 'large quantity' (*Dr. Moreland's lecture was 3 carriages of coal for the brain*), 'energy' (*Dr. Moreland's lecture was like a sparkle that set my mind on fire*), or 'pleasure' (*Dr. Moreland's lecture was a bunch of flower for a spinster*). In other words, the conceptual metaphor view failed to provide a framework within which one could account for the metaphorical expressions produced by Polish learners of English. While the attributive categorization view turned out to be more successful in explaining some of such expressions, it too failed to account for the strategies underlying the comprehension and interpretation of more difficult metaphorical stimuli. These results should be interpreted with caution, though. Requesting paraphrases from subjects sets a task which relies exclusively on post-access interpretation strategies and cannot be taken to reflect on-line mechanisms of metaphor comprehension. Lack of conceptual metaphor-consistent paraphrases in the data does not preclude the possibility that conceptual metaphors are activated in the course of bilingual figurative language processing. They might be active in the processing of verbal metaphors and even play some role in arriving at the interpretation of a metaphorical expression, but fail to surface in the written paraphrases of such an expression. Whether and to what extent conceptual metaphors are activated during on-line bilingual processing of metaphorical language remains to be determined by future research.

Metaphors and L2 instruction

With regard to the role of instruction, Kovesces and Szabó (1996) show that the learning of idioms can be facilitated by explicit instruction about the conceptual motivation for the meaning of idioms. They conducted an informal experiment in which they taught a set of English phrasal verbs to two groups of Hungarian students. One group simply saw the phrasal verbs on the blackboard along with their Hungarian equivalents and were simply asked to memorize them, while another group were first instructed in the orientational metaphors motivating the phrasal verbs' meanings (e.g. COMPLETION IS UP, motivating *eat up*; or LACK OF CONTROL IS DOWN, motivating *knock down*). Subsequently, both groups were given a completion task consisting of 20 sentences containing phrasal verbs in which *up* or *down* were omitted. While some of the sentences contained phrasal verbs presented previously, unknown phrasal verbs were also included, these latter being motivated by the same conceptual metaphors as the phrasal verbs presented in the learning phase. Learners were required to insert the missing particle in each sentence. It transpired that the group taught with the help of conceptual metaphors performed much better than the group which memorized the phrasal verbs without further conceptual metaphor explanation, this advantage holding for the sentences containing both the previously introduced and the unknown phrasal verbs.

This idea was also explored by Boers (2000). He asked two groups of Dutch learners of English to read a text containing figurative expressions. After reading the text, the experimental group received vocabulary notes organized around metaphorical themes that underlay new figurative expressions in the text. The control group received the same vocabulary input, but organized along pragmatic and functional lines. Both groups were given time to familiarize themselves with the notes and were then given a cloze test, from which some of the learned items had been deleted. It emerged that students from the experimental group were more likely than those from the control group to fill gaps correctly. In a further experiment, Boers presented learners of English with vocabulary items describing upward and downward economic trends (e.g. *to soar, to plunge*, etc.) While the experimental group received explanations referring to the source domains of the economic expressions, the control group simply received explanations of the words' meanings. After the learning phase, students were asked to write a short essay describing the changes represented by graphs depicting economic trends in various countries and were encouraged to employ the terms they had just learned. Analysis revealed that the experimental group had used many more of the learned figurative items than the control group. In a third experiment, Boers replicated Kovesces and Szabó's (1996) experiment (see above) and found that students who had studied verbs categorized under conceptual metaphors were more likely to fill in the gaps correctly in the completion test than students without explicit instruction in the orientational metaphors. However, this advantage held true only for the sentences containing previously introduced verbs. The above results corroborate the view that L2 learners can benefit considerably from an enhanced awareness of conceptual metaphors. On the other hand, Boers observes that most of the expressions employed in his experiments were semantically transparent and that metaphor awareness may be 'less fruitful when the learner is faced with opaque idioms' (Boers, 2000: 563) with respect to which he suggests exploiting their historico-cultural background (cf. Deignan, Gabryś and Solska 1997).

The role of cross-cultural comparisons of conceptual metaphors motivating figurative expressions is further explored by Charteris-Black (2002), who claims that the identification of conceptual and linguistic similarities and differences between L1 and L2 figurative expressions enables one to anticipate potential problems in the acquisition of L2 figurative language. To explore the influence of different figurative expression-types on learners' performance, he conducted a comprehension and production test with Malay learners of English. Analysis of learners' performance on both tasks showed that figurative expressions with equivalent linguistic forms and an equivalent conceptual basis were the easiest to process. The most difficult expressions turned out to be those with an equivalent linguistic form and a different conceptual basis, as well as culture-specific expressions with a different linguistic form and a different conceptual basis. These findings, according to Charteris-Black, point to the necessity of drawing students' attention to conceptual metaphors when they differ for L1 and L2 figurative expressions. With expressions sharing common conceptual bases, it appears necessary to focus on linguistic differences.

Concluding remarks

It is clear that the conceptual metaphor view of figurative language processing remains controversial. Strong evidence has been adduced in its favour in the L1 domain, but one can also point to a body of counter-evidence, as well as a number of question-marks regarding its theoretical coherence. The L2 evidence likewise presents a rather mixed picture. Despite the criticisms that have been levelled against it, however, the conceptual metaphor view has been extremely influential and has self-evidently motivated invaluable research into the structure of concepts, the nature of human cognition and the mechanisms of language comprehension.

With regard to the possible benefits of applying metaphor research findings in the L2 classroom, the results of a number of studies discussed above suggest that raising learners' consciousness about the conceptual motivation of linguistic metaphors in the L2 leads to improved performance in the processing and retention of the metaphors in question. It is noteworthy that the studies in question were conducted under the auspices of the conceptual metaphor view, although their findings are also compatible with less theory-specific notions concerning the positive role that can be played in lexical learning by the raising of consciousness about meaning-related dimensions and commonalities of novel expressions.

In sum, while the conceptual metaphor view will no doubt continue to be a matter of debate, the kinds of pedagogical practices it has inspired appear to lead to real improvements in learners' apprehension and assimilation of L2 linguistic metaphor. Perhaps other models of metaphorical processing might be drawn on in a similar fashion for approaches that might be explored in the classroom. Further insights gleaned from a wider range of theoretical proposals might lead to the development of a broader array of techniques, promoting even more successful enhancement of L2 learners' metaphorical competence.

References

Alexander, R.J. (1987) 'Problems in Understanding and Teaching Idiomaticity in English', *Anglistik und Englischunterricht*, **32**, 105-122.

Allbritton, D.W., McKoon, G. and Gerrig R.J. (1995) 'Metaphor-Based Schemas and Text Representations: Making Connections through Conceptual Metaphors', *Journal of Experimental Psychology: Learning, Memory, and Cognition*, **21**, 3, 612-625.

Boers, F. (2000) 'Metaphor Awareness and Vocabulary Retention', *Applied Linguistics*, **21**, 4, 553-571.

Bortfeld, H. (2002) 'What Native and Non-Native Speakers' Images for Idioms Tell Us about Figurative Language', in R. R. Heredia and J. Altarriba (eds.), *Bilingual Sentence Processing*, 275-295, Elsevier: Amsterdam.

Camac, M. K. and Glucksberg, S. (1984) 'Metaphors do not Use Associations between Concepts, They are Used to Create Them', *Journal of Psycholinguistic Research*, **13**, 6, 443-455.

Charteris-Black, J. (2002) 'Second Language Figurative Proficiency: A Comparative Study of Malay and English', *Applied Linguistics*, **23**, 1, 104-133.

Cieślicka, A. (2002) 'Metaphors of Teaching and Learning: Investigating Bilingual Metaphorical Competence', in D. Stanulewicz (ed.), *PASE Papers in Language Studies: Proceedings of the Ninth Annual Conference of the Polish Association for the Study of English, Gdansk, 26-28 April 2000*, 383-392, Wydawnictwo Uniwersytetu Gdanskiego: Gdansk.

Cieślicka, A. (2003) 'On Understanding Metaphorical Expressions in the Bilingual Mode', *Linguistica Silesiana*, **24**, 143-168.

Clark, E. (1993) *The Lexicon in Acquisition*, Cambridge University Press: Cambridge.

Cortazzi, M. and Jin, L (1999) 'Bridges to Learning: Metaphors of Teaching, Learning and Language', in L. Cameron and G. Low (eds.), *Researching and Applying Metaphor*, 149-176, Cambridge University Press: Cambridge.

Danesi, M. (1992) 'Metaphorical Competence in Second Language Acquisition and Second Language Teaching: The Neglected Dimension', in J. E. Alatis (ed.), *Georgetown University Round Table on Languages and Linguistics*, 489-500, Georgetown University Press: Washington, DC.

Deignan, A., Gabryś, D. and Solska, A. (1997) 'Teaching English Metaphors Using Cross-Linguistic Awareness-Raising Activities', *ELT Journal*, 51, 4, 352-360.

Elliot, A. (1981) *Child Language*, Cambridge University Press: Cambridge.

Gibbs, R.W. (1994) 'Categorization and Metaphor Understanding', *Psychological Review*, 99, 3, 572-577.

Gibbs, R.W. (1994) *The Poetics of Mind: Figurative Thought, Language and Understanding*, Cambridge University Press: Cambridge.

Gibbs, R.W. (1996) 'Why many Concepts are Metaphorical', *Cognition*, 61, 309-319.

Gibbs, R.W. (1998) 'The Fight over Metaphor in Thought and Language', in A.N. Katz, C. Cacciari, R.W. Gibbs and M. Turner (eds.), *Figurative Language and Thought*, 88-118, Oxford University Press: Oxford.

Gibbs, R.W. (1999) 'Taking Metaphor out of our Heads and Putting it into the Cultural World', in R. W. Gibbs and G. J. Steen (eds.), *Metaphor in Cognitive Linguistics: Selected Papers from the Fifth International Cognitive Linguistics Conference, Amsterdam, July 1997*, 145-166, John Benjamins Publishing Company: Amsterdam/Philadelphia.

Gibbs, R.W. (2001) 'Evaluating Contemporary Models of Figurative Language Understanding', *Metaphor and Symbol*, 16, 3 and 4, 317-333.

Gibbs, R.W. and Beitel, D. (1995) 'What Proverb Understanding Reveals about How People Think', *Psychological Bulletin*, 118, 1, 133-154.

Gibbs, R.W. and Kearney, L.R. (1994) 'When Parting is Such Sweet Sorrow: The Comprehension and Appreciation of Oxymora', *Journal of Psycholinguistic Research*, 23, 1, 75-89.

Gibbs, R.W. and O'Brien, J. (1990) 'Idioms and Mental Imagery: The Metaphorical Motivation for Idiomatic Meaning', *Cognition*, 36, 35-68.

Gibbs, R.W., Strom, L.K. and Spivey-Knowlton, M.J. (1997) 'Conceptual Metaphors in Mental Imagery for Proverbs', *Journal of Mental Imagery*, 21, 3 and 4, 83-110.

Glucksberg, S. (1991) 'Beyond Literal Meanings: The Psychology of Allusion', *Psychological Science*, 2, 3, 146-152.

Glucksberg, S. (1995) 'Commentary on Nonliteral Language: Processing and Use', *Metaphor and Symbolic Activity*, 10, 1, 47-57.

Glucksberg, S. (2001) *Understanding Figurative Language: From Metaphors to Idioms*, Oxford University Press: New York.

Glucksberg, S., Gildea, P. and Bookin, H. B. (1982) 'On Understanding Nonliteral Speech: Can People Ignore Metaphors?', *Journal of Verbal Learning and Verbal*

Behavior, **21**, 85-98.

Glucksberg, S. and Keysar, B. (1990) 'Understanding Metaphorical Comparisons: Beyond Similarity', *Psychological Review,* **97**, 1, 3-18.

Glucksberg, S., Keysar, B. and McGlone, M.S. (1992) 'Metaphor Understanding and Accessing Conceptual Schema: Reply to Gibbs (1992)', *Psychological Review,* **99**, 3, 578-581.

Glucksberg, S., and McGlone, M.S. (1999) 'When Love is not a Journey: What Metaphors Mean', *Journal of Pragmatics,* **31**, 1541-1558.

Glucksberg, S., McGlone, M. S. and Manfredi, D. (1997) 'Property Attribution in Metaphor Comprehension', *Journal of Memory and Language,* **36**, 50-67.

Glucksberg, S., Newsome, M. R. and Goldvarg, Y. (2001) 'Inhibition of the Literal: Filtering Metaphor-Irrelevant Information during Metaphor Comprehension', *Metaphor and Symbol,* **16**, 3 and 4, 277-293.

Hobbes, T. (1962) *Leviathan,* (ed.) John Plamenatz, London: Collins, original date of publication 1651.

Irujo, S. (1993) 'Steering Clear: Avoidance in the Production of Idioms', *IRAL,* **31**, 3, 205-219.

Kecskes, I. and Papp, T. (2000) 'Metaphorical Competence in Trilingual Language Production', in J. Cenoz and U. Jessner (eds.), *English in Europe: The Acquisition of a Third Language,* 99-120, Multilingual Matters Ltd., Clevedon.

Kovecses, Z. (1986), *Metaphors of Anger, Pride, and Love,* John Benjamins, Philadelphia.

Kovescses, Z. and Szabó, P. (1996) 'Idioms: A View from Cognitive Semantics', *Applied Linguistics,* **17**, 3, 326-355.

Lakoff, G. (1987) *Women, Fire, and Dangerous Things,* Chicago University Press: Chicago.

Lakoff, G. (1990) 'The Invariance Hypothesis: Is Abstract Reasoning Based on Image-Schemas?', *Cognitive Linguistics,* **1**, 1, 39-74.

Lakoff, G. (1993) 'The Contemporary Theory of Metaphor', in A. Ortony (ed.), *Metaphor and Thought,* Cambridge University Press: New York.

Lakoff, G. and Johnson, M. (1980) *Metaphors We Live By,* Chicago University Press: Chicago.

Lakoff, G. and Turner, M. (1989) *More than Cool Reason: A Field Guide to Poetic Metaphor,* University of Chicago Press: Chicago.

Lattey, E. (1986) 'Pragmatic Classification of Idioms as an Aid for the Language Learner', *IRAL,* **24**, 3, 217-233.

Levorato, M.C. (1993) 'The Acquisition of Idioms and the Development of Figurative Competence', in C. Cacciari and P. Tabossi (eds.), *Idioms: Processing, Structure, and Interpretation,* 101-128, Lawrence Erlbaum Associates: Hillsdale, NJ.

Low, G.D. (1988) 'On Teaching Metaphor', *Applied Linguistics,* **9**, 125-147.

McGlone, M.S. (1996) 'Conceptual Metaphors and Figurative Language Interpretation: Food for Thought?', *Journal of Memory and Language,* **35**, 544-565.

Moon, R., (1997) 'Vocabulary Connections: Multi-Word Items in English', in N.

Schmitt and M. McCarthy (eds.), *Vocabulary: Description, Acquisition and Pedagogy*, 40-63, Cambridge University Press: Cambridge.

Murphy, G. L. (1996) 'On Metaphoric Representation', *Cognition*, **60**, 173-204.

Murphy, G. L. (1997) 'Reasons to Doubt the Present Evidence for Metaphoric Representation', *Cognition*, **62**, 99-108.

Nayak, N. P. and Gibbs, R. W. (1990) 'Conceptual Knowledge in the Interpretation of Idioms', *Journal of Experimental Psychology: General*, **119**, 3, 315-330.

Pfaff, K. L., Gibbs, R.W. and Johnson, M. D. (1997) 'Metaphor in Using and Understanding Euphemism and Dysphemism', *Applied Psycholinguistics*, **18**, 59-83.

Richards, I. A. (1936) *The Philosophy of Rhetoric*, Oxford University Press: Oxford.

Singleton, D. (1999) *Exploring the Second Language Mental Lexicon*, Cambridge University Press: Cambridge.

Singleton, D. and Ryan, L. (forthcoming) *Language Acquisition: The Age Factor*, Second Edition, Multilingual Matters: Clevedon.

Winner, E. (1997) *Point of Words: Children's Understanding of Metaphor and Irony*, Harvard University Press: Cambridge, MA.

Zughoul, M.R. (1991) 'Lexical Choice: Towards Writing Problematic Word Lists', *IRAL*, **29**, 1, 45-60.

V_LINKS: BEYOND VOCABULARY DEPTH

PAUL MEARA AND BRENT WOLTER

ABSTRACT

This paper argues that the distinction made by many people between vocabulary breadth and vocabulary depth is an unfortunate one. Although the dichotomy is appealing, it forces us to look at vocabulary development in an unhelpful way. Depth of vocabulary knowledge can only be assessed by means of more and more detailed tests and the logistics of testing implies that this work can be done only with fewer and fewer words. The paper argues that **vocabulary size** and **vocabulary organisation** is a much more productive way of looking at vocabularies. It outlines some of our work on vocabulary organisation, and reports some preliminary results with a tool designed to assess the way core vocabularies are organised in L2 speakers.

Introduction

Recent work on vocabulary acquisition has tended to make a broad distinction between **vocabulary breadth** and **vocabulary depth**. Vocabulary breadth has generally been interpreted as the number of words that learners know, whereas vocabulary depth is generally taken to mean how well they know these words. Most of the research in this framework goes back to a seminal article by Richards published in 1976, though the ideas have been picked up and developed by other writers since that time (e.g. Nation 1990, Nation 2001, af Trampe 1983; Blum-Kulka 1981; Madden 1980, McNeill 1996, and others). Richards' paper identifies a number of different aspects of word knowledge and the most important of these are summarised in Figure 1.

- Knowing a word means knowing the degree of probability of encountering a word in speech or print. For many words we also know the sort of words most likely to be found associated with the word.
- Knowing a word implies knowing the limitations imposed on the use of the word according to variations of function and situation.
- Knowing a word means knowing the syntactic behaviour associated with a word.
- Knowing a word entails knowledge of the underlying form of the word and the derivatives that can be made from it.
- Knowing a word entails knowledge of the network of associations between the word and the other words in the language.
- Knowing a word means knowing the semantic value of word.
- Knowing a word means knowing many of the different meanings associated with the word. (P 83).

Figure 1. Aspects of word knowledge from Richards (1976)

A number of people have tried to develop formal tests which measure depth of vocabulary knowledge in these terms. Wesche and Paribakht (1996) for instance developed a rating scale approach, in which test-takers are invited to rate their knowledge of target words on a five point scale, generating definitions for the target words or sentences containing the target words to confirm their self-ratings where appropriate. Although VKS was initially developed as a way of measuring specific gains in vocabulary as a result of reading, it has often been taken as a more general test for measuring depth of vocabulary knowledge. A further example of this approach is Schmitt and Meara (1997). This paper developed an instrument which assessed test-takers' ability to generate derivative forms of target words, attempting to show that this ability was independent of vocabulary breadth. Other examples of vocabulary depth tests, which adopt the same general approach include Schmitt (1994) and Read (1995).

This work clearly takes the idea of 'knowing a word' some way further than the measures of vocabulary breadth which are currently available. These latter measures tend to be relatively superficial: Meara's Yes/No tests, for example (Meara and Milton 2003) simply ask test-takers to say whether they can recognise that a word exists or not, and Nation's Vocabulary Levels Test (Nation 2001; Schmitt, Schmitt and Clapham 2001) requires test-takers merely to match words to simple definitions. The depth tests, in contrast, require test-takers to show that their knowledge of the target words is not limited to superficial knowledge of this sort.

It seems to us, however, that this enterprise is fundamentally doomed. The problem is that testing vocabulary depth in this way requires us to carry out extensive testing of individual words, and this makes it all but impossible to design experiments which can tell us very much about the larger characteristics of whole vocabularies – a classic example of not being able to see the wood for looking at the trees. The logic of testing vocabulary depth using the vocabulary knowledge framework implies that we need to test very many words in ever-increasing detail, and this very quickly leads us into serious logistical problems which constrain the types of hypotheses that we can test. Suppose, for example, that we take Richards' list at face value, and suppose that we want to test how well a group of L2 speakers knows a list of 50 target words. To carry out this work, we would need to develop a set of perhaps a dozen subtests for each of the words we are interested in – at least one subtest for each feature in the framework. If we want to test 50 words in this way, then this implies that we would need a minimum of 600 test items before we can make even basic statements about a student's depth of vocabulary knowledge for these words. And this in turn assumes that we could develop a single test item able to assess depth of knowledge in a meaningful way. On purely logistic grounds, a test battery of this size is completely infeasible: in practical terms, it would be very difficult indeed to get large groups of learners to take a 600 item test. In any case, it is highly unlikely that we could develop single test items that would reliably access a learner's depth of knowledge for target words – it is very difficult to think of any way of testing how well a learner knows the syntactic behaviour of a word using a single test item, for instance – and this implies that we would actually need several test items for each of the facets listed in Figure 1. A 'solution' which involved even more test items would result in even larger and even less feasible tests, this in turn implies that we must reduce dramatically the number of target words we test. Suppose, then, that we reduce our hypothetical list of target words to 10 items, and suppose that we develop a set of 20 sub-tests for each word. Even a minimal list of this sort would still require a battery of 200 subtests, and the nature of the material would probably require each subtest to be separately developed and validated. This does not feel like an attractive proposition to us. Furthermore, even if a testing program of this sort could be developed and deployed, we would still be left with the far from negligible problem of how we can generalise from our 10 target words to the rest of the vocabulary.

Put in its simplest terms, then, the prevailing approach to depth of vocabulary knowledge requires us to develop more and more finely tuned tests for fewer and fewer words. We do not think that this is a productive way to go, and our own thinking has led us in a rather different direction. Most people would agree that the recent growth in vocabulary research has largely been driven by the development of simple tests for vocabulary breadth – though for reasons which will become clear later, we prefer to call it **vocabulary size**. Typically in a test of this sort we give the test takers a large number of words and evaluate whether they 'know' these words or not. At first sight, this work looks as though we are primarily concerned with single words, but actually things are more complicated than this. If the target words are well-chosen, then we can extrapolate from the target words to an estimate of the test-taker's overall vocabulary size, and most tests of vocabulary breadth do just this. Thus, although we are ostensibly testing individual words, what really interests us is using this data to generate a description of the test takers' overall vocabulary size. **Vocabulary size** is not a feature of individual words: rather it is a characteristic of the test taker's entire vocabulary. This is a subtle shift of focus but an important one, and it has considerable implications for the way we approach measures of vocabulary depth.

We believe that the attempts made by researchers such as Wesche and Paribakht, and Schmitt focus in too much detail on knowledge of individual words, and neglect the larger picture. We believe that a better approach to vocabulary development would be to look at features which are characteristic of a learner's whole lexicon, rather than features which are characteristic only of single words. Ideally what we would like is a characteristic which scales in much the same way as vocabulary size measures scale. Vocabulary size is a good measure, with highly desirable measurement characteristics: vocabulary size measures start at zero, and they have a wide range, typically several thousand, and this means that they are very easy to work with, and very easy to interpret. Ideally we would like to develop a 'depth' characteristic with similar features.

An alternative to breadth and depth

Our current view is that depth of vocabulary knowledge is rather more than the sum of the learners' knowledge of the individual words in their vocabulary. Knowledge of individual words contributes to depth of knowledge, but the really interesting feature of vocabularies is the way that the individual words that make them up interact with each other. These interactions are what distinguish between a mere **vocabulary list** and a **vocabulary network**. The basic idea, one that has been widely taken up by writers on vocabulary acquisition, e.g Aitchison (1987) and McCarthy (1990), is that words in a vocabulary form some kind of linked network. Aitchison, for example, refers to a lexicon as 'a gigantic multi-dimensional cobweb' (p72), while McCarthy talks in very similar terms. Although these authors do not develop these metaphors in any detail, we believe that we can approach the question of vocabulary depth by characterising the properties of this network rather than by focussing on the properties of its separate components. The difference between this view of vocabulary depth and the more traditional view is summarised in Figure 2.

The left hand diagram in Figure 2 illustrates the way vocabulary breadth and vocabulary depth are currently conceptualised. Each word is shown as a bar. Words with more 'depth' are shown as longer bars, while words with less 'depth' are shown as shorter bars. Essentially, this is a list model. Adding new words (increasing breadth) has no implications for the other words in the list, and there is no intrinsic link between breadth and depth.

The right hand diagram shows a more complex, network metaphor. In this model, 'breadth', or size, corresponds to the number of nodes in the network. The second dimension of this feature is the number of connections between the nodes. For this model, adding a new node (increasing 'breadth')

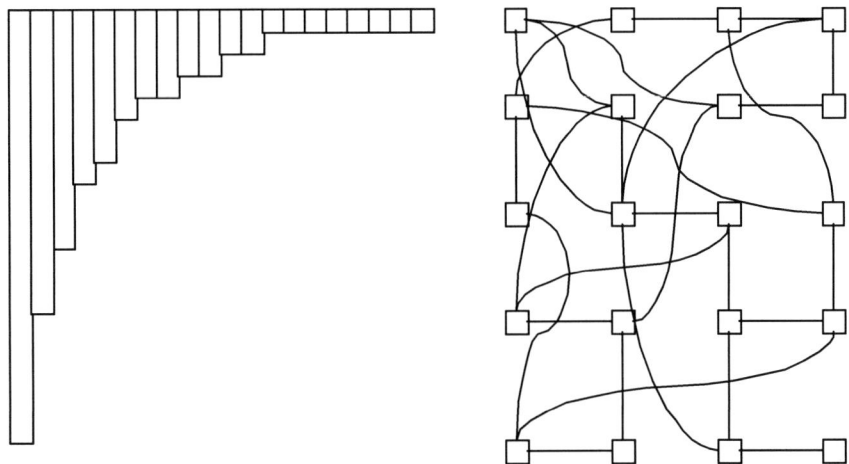

Figure 2. Two ways of looking at a vocabulary

does have implications for the rest of the network, depending on how the new node is linked to the existing ones. Adding new links (increasing 'depth') also has implications for the rest of the network.

The two metaphors are fundamentally different, and lead us to ask very different questions about the way 'breadth' and 'depth', or in our terms, **size** and **organisation**, interact. Basically, we think that the breadth/depth opposition is an unfortunate one, that leads in unhelpful directions. We believe that it makes more sense to talk about size and structure or size and organisation instead.

Our own research has been based on the idea that L2 lexicons are not as highly structured as the lexicons of L1 speakers. This seems like an intuitively plausible place to start: everyone agrees that L1 lexicons are highly developed and complex, while L2 lexicons are less well developed. In terms of our model, this should mean that L2 lexicons are smaller than L1 lexicons, and that the organisational links between the words that make up the L2 lexicon should be simpler than what we find in L1 lexicons.

The obvious way to investigate these ideas is to use word association data. In experiments of this sort, we give L2 speakers a series of single words, and we ask them to report the first L2 word that comes into their heads. We can then assume that the reported associations are linked in much the same way as the nodes in Figure 2 are linked. We might expect native speaker networks developed in this way to be denser and more highly organised than similar networks generated by L2 speakers, and this would suggest that the complexity of the connections between words corresponds in some way to vocabulary 'depth'. Words which show a complex array of connections will tend to be more deeply known than words which are linked more tenuously to other words. This deceptively simple idea turns out to be much harder to work with than you would expect. Word associations generated by L2 speakers are quite different from those produced by L1 speakers (cf. Riegel and Zivian 1972), but the differences are very hard to pin down reliably in small scale experiments. This is largely because L2 speakers seem to produce a much wider range of associations than L1 speakers do, but it is also difficult to disentangle the effects of L1 interference in L2 word association tasks.

Most word association research relies on a methodology which requires test-takers to produce associations, and this tends to generate data which is particularly varied, and particularly difficult to work with. However, Wilks and Meara (2002) developed a sophisticated passive association recognition technique which allowed them to estimate the mean number of associational links between small sets of words. Their data showed that there were clear differences between native speakers and L2 speakers in this regard. In their approach, test-takers were provided with small sets of words and asked to decide whether any two words in each set were associated together. Not surprisingly, L1 speakers were more likely to find a link than L2 speakers were. Wilks and Meara computed the probability of a link being found for these sets, and then used a complex modelling method to estimate the complexity of the connections in their subjects' lexicons.

The work we report in the next section of this paper is basically a development of Wilks and Meara's methodology.

V_Links

The testing tools that we describe in this section are a preliminary attempt to develop a measure of lexical organisation for English. The test is known as V_Links, and its current version is version 2.00. The test consists of a set of 20 items. Each item consists of a selection of 10 words. The words all come from the first 1000 words in English. The test items were developed from a larger number of randomly selected word sets so that each set contains a number of obvious and some less obvious associational pairs. The test-takers are presented with each of these 20 items on a computer screen, and for each item they are given one minute to identify any association pairs that they can find. They do this by clicking on the words in the display. Each pair is confirmed when the test takers indicate how strong the association is by clicking on a four point scale at the bottom of the display. The display

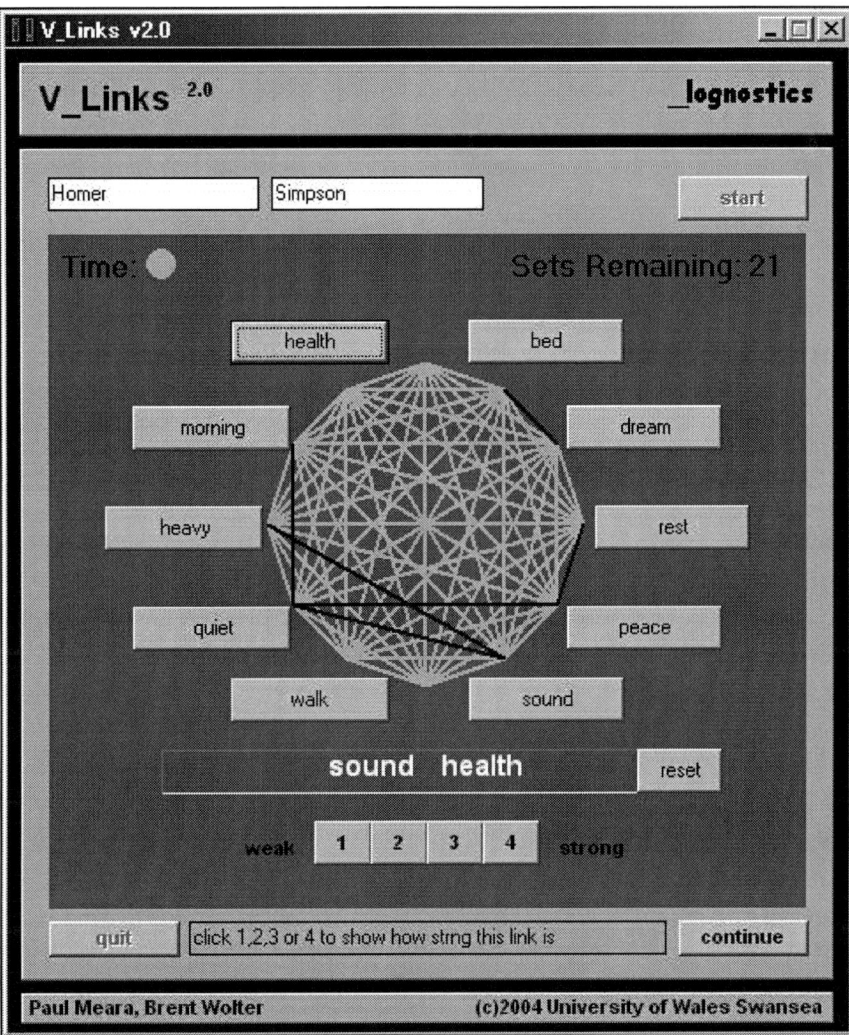

Figure 3. Screen shot from V_Links

then draws a link between the two members of the pair, with the strength of the display shown by differences in the line colour. (See Figure 3).

We have trialled this basic idea in a several different formats and the current version of our test works reasonably well. This version has a number of interesting features.

Firstly, it tests a large number of words in a relatively short space of time. Each of our 20 items contains 10 target words, so the whole test features a total of 200 words – one in five of the basic 1000 word core vocabulary. This figure is much larger than anything that could be attempted using an approach like VKS, and we think it gives us much greater insight into the way a vocabulary is organised than a smaller test could. In spite of this, the test takes only 30 minutes to administer.

Secondly, each item has a possible 45 linked pairs, though in practice, the actual number of pairs identified is much smaller than this. Native speakers typically identify half a dozen word pairs as associational pairs for each item. Multiplying this up across all twenty items gives us a total of 120 providing us with a scale ranging from 0-120. This range seems to be large enough to clearly distinguish between native speakers and learners.

Thirdly, the fact that the test makes use only of words which lie in the first thousand frequency band for English means that the test in its current form can be used with test takers whose level of English varies over a considerable range of proficiency. Obviously, the test is not suitable for absolute beginners who have a very limited vocabulary, but it can be used with intermediate level learners, as well as advanced level learners, and the data we have collected so far suggests that the test may be sensitive enough to discriminate clearly between these cases.

There are, of course, a number of outstanding problems which we still need to address, and these form the object of our current work with the test format. The most important of these problems is that our L2 test takers persistently identify as associates word pairs which are never selected by native speaker test takers. We had originally hoped that these cases would be few, and that we would be able to ignore them, but this appears not to be the case. Our current approach to this problem has been to build up a database of the responses produced by a group of L1 speakers, and to accept as valid any response which appears more than once in this set – i.e. at least two native speaker respondents have made this association. This is not entirely satisfactory, as it fails to take account of L2 associations which arise as a result of specific local conditions – English loan-words used as trade names in Japan are a particular problem in this context – but in principle, the methodology could be adapted to take account of special cases such as these. Using a response database allows us to score the test automatically, and to provide instant feedback to test-takers.

The second problem is the question of association strength. In our earlier versions of V_Links, we asked test-takers to identify any associated pairs, but did not ask them to say how strong or how obvious the association was. This made the task easy for the test-takers, but it sometimes produced data which was difficult to interpret. Some test-takers, for example, would claim there was an association between a pair like COW and SNAIL, on the grounds that both were animals, or between LOOK and WRITE on the grounds that both were verbs. In our current version of V_Links, test-takers have to indicate how strong they think each of their associations is, and we hope that this will allow us to weed out some of the more unsatisfactory associations in a principled way. Most people, for example, think that the association between DOG and CAT is stronger than the association between COW and SNAIL, and most people think that WRITE ~ PEN is a stronger association than WRITE ~ LOOK. However, this approach has thrown up other problems which we have not yet solved, notably a tendency for some test takers to claim that most associations are strong, while others appear to be very reluctant to use only the lower end of our four-point scale.

The third problem that we are still working on is the question of timing. Ideally, we would like to have a measure of vocabulary organisation which is independent of other factors, such as speed of word recognition and fluency. For this reason, some of our earlier versions of V_Links did not impose any time limit on the test-takers, and used an open-ended format instead. This worked well with some speakers, but others seemed to take a perverse delight in exploring all the possible combinations of words in each set, and finding obscure links between them. We have reintroduced a timer into the current version, with the time allowed for each test item being amply sufficient for test takers to identify the most obvious associations. It is possible that this makes the test harder for students whose reading speed is poor, but we do not think so. A more important factor seems to be how fluent test-takers are in using a mouse, and we think that this problem will disappear as more and more people are accustomed to this mode of working with a computer.

Does V_Links work?

The format we have described in this paper is the latest in a long series of trial versions which we have been working on for some time. V_Links clearly discriminates between native speakers and non-native speakers. In a large scale trial involving 147 L1-Japanese learners of English, the test showed a significant difference between these learners and a control group of native speakers, with the L2-speakers scoring about half the mean score for native speakers ($t = 3.25$, $p < .01$). We expect that our current version of V_Links will perform even better than this early trial version.

Data from the same group of subjects also suggests that there is only a very modest level of correlation between scores on the V_Links test and scores on a test of overall vocabulary size ($r < 0.3$), and this is exactly what we would expect if lexical organisation and size are more-or-less independent features of L2 lexicons. Clearly, further work on this is needed, and we will be carrying out more studies of this sort when we have finalised the current version of V-Links.

Further work with V_Links

In the earlier sections of this paper, we argued that the size/organisation approach to L2 vocabularies was potentially more productive than the breadth/depth approach. In this section, we will explore this idea in more detail.

The size/organisation approach to vocabulary development is part of a multi-dimensional approach to L2 vocabularies that was first outlined in Meara (1996). Meara argued that both size and organisation were important characteristics which impacted on lexical behaviour. We have had reliable tests for measuring vocabulary size for some time. If we are right in thinking that V_Links is an effective way of assessing lexical organisation, then we now have tests for measuring these two basic dimensions in place, and this allows us to start asking some really interesting questions about the relationship between vocabulary size and vocabulary organisation. The basic question we can ask is whether organisation and size are correlated – i.e. whether the core vocabulary (the most frequent 1000 words) of a large lexicon is more structured than the same words are when they are part of a small lexicon. As we have seen, our preliminary results suggest that there is not a straightforward correlation between vocabulary size and vocabulary organisation. The question that then arises is just what is the relationship? Is it completely random or is it a complex non-linear relationship? The answer to this question is by no means obvious. There are, however, a number of plausible ways in which size and organisation might be related in a non-linear fashion.

One possibility is that people with similar sized vocabularies might differ in respect of how organised they are, i.e. we might find learners with similar vocabulary sizes, but very different degrees of organisation in their lexicons. If this turned out to be the case, then we might begin to ask how the different learner types identified by the dimensional approach differ in their language behaviour. We might expect learners with large, but weakly organised lexicons to behave differently from learners with similarly sized, but better organised lexicons - perhaps they would be less good at text comprehension, for example, or less good at understanding extended spoken input.

Another possibility is that lexical organisation may be an insignificant factor as long as the lexicons in question are below a critical size threshold, but that organisation becomes increasingly important once this critical size is reached. For example, it might be the case that small lexicons show a wide disparity in organisation, while large lexicons are always highly organised. This idea in turn suggests that there might be a number of thresholds of this sort, and this would imply a complex relationship between size and organisation. Perhaps unstructured, or loosely structured lexicons can only grow to a limit, and cannot grow beyond this limit until they have restructured themselves. This would imply that lexicons might have growth phases and consolidation phases. We cannot think of any empirical work which supports this suggestion. However, it does fit well with some anecdotal accounts of vocabulary acquisition in L2 learners implying that learners feel their vocabulary reaches a sort of plateau from which it is difficult to make further progress.

V_Links should allow us to investigate these questions by carrying out detailed longitudinal studies designed to work out how vocabulary size and vocabulary organisation are related over time. Work of this sort would also indicate how far different learners follow the same trajectory in the space defined by our twin dimensions. At the moment, we have very little idea how much learners vary in the way their vocabularies are organised, and almost no idea how lexical organisation might facilitate further lexical growth, or how it might impact on other aspects of language performance. However, we expect to find considerable individual differences between learners in this respect, and if this turns out to be the case, then tests like V_Links will play an increasingly important role in vocabulary research.

Conclusion

In this paper, we have described our current thinking abut lexical organisation, and shown how measures of vocabulary organisation offer a more interesting approach to the question of vocabulary development than the idea of 'vocabulary depth' does. We have described the current version of our tool, **V_Links**, and some of the preliminary investigations we have carried out using this tool. V_Links still has a way to go before it is fully functional, but we hope that this brief description of our current work will convince readers that the type of approach embodied in V_Links has the potential to open up some seriously interesting avenues in vocabulary research.

References

af Trampe, P. (1983) 'Foreign Language Learning - a Criterion of Learning Achievement', in H. Ringbom (ed.), *Psycholinguistics and Foreign Language Learning,* Åbo Akademi: Åbo.

Aitchison, J. (1987) *Words in the Mind,* Blackwell: Oxford.

Blum-Kulka, S. (1981) 'Learning to Use Words: Acquiring Semantic Competence in a Second Language', in M. Nahir (ed.), *Hebrew Teaching and Applied Linguistics*, University Press of America: New York.

Madden, J. F. (1980) 'Developing Pupils' Vocabulary Skills', *Guidelines* **3**, 111-117.

McNeill, A. (1996) 'Vocabulary Knowledge Profiles: Evidence from Chinese-Speaking ESL Teachers', *Hong Kong Journal of Applied Linguistics*, **1**, 39-64.

McCarthy, M. (1990) *Vocabulary*, Oxford University Press: Oxford.

Meara, P.M. (1996) 'The Dimensions of Lexical Competence', in Brown, G., Malmkjaer, K. and J. Williams (eds.), *Performance and Competence in Second Language Acquisition*, 35-53, Cambridge University Press: Cambridge.

Meara, P. M. and Milton, J.L. (2003) *X_Lex: the Swansea Vocabulary Levels Test*, Swansea: Lognostics.

Nation, I. S. P. (1990) *Teaching and Learning Vocabulary*, Heinle and Heinle: Boston.

Nation, I. S. P. (2001) *Learning Vocabulary in Another Language*, Cambridge University Press: Cambridge.

Read, J. (1995) 'Refining the Word Associates Format as a Measure of Depth of Vocabulary Knowledge', *New Zealand Studies in Applied Linguistics*, **1**, 1-17.

Riegel, K. F. and Zivian, I. W. M. (1972) 'A Study of Inter- and Intralingual Associations in English and German', *Language Learning*, **22**, 1, 51-63.

Richards, J. C. (1976) 'The Role of Vocabulary Teaching', *TESOL Quarterly*, **10**, 77-89.

Schmitt, N. (1994) 'Vocabulary Testing: Questions for Test Development with Six Examples of Tests of Vocabulary Size and Depth', *Thai TESOL Bulletin*, **6**, 2, 9-16.

Schmitt, N. and Meara, P. M. (1997) 'Researching Vocabulary through a Word Knowledge Framework: Word Associations and Verbal Suffixes', *Studies in Second Language Acquisition*, **19**, 1, 17-36.

Schmitt, N., Schmitt, D. and Clapham, C. (2001) 'Developing and Exploring the Behaviour of Two New Versions of the Vocabulary Levels Test', *Language Testing*, **18**, 1, 55-89.

Wesche, M. and Paribakht, T. S. (1996) 'Assessing Vocabulary Knowledge: Depth vs. Breadth', *Canadian Modern Language Review*, **53**, 1, 13-40.

Wilks, C. and Meara, P. M. (2002) 'Untangling Word Webs: Graph Theory and the Notion of Density in Second Language Word Association Networks', *Second Language Research*, **18**, 4, 303-324.

Copies of V_Links v 2.00 are available from http://www.swansea.ac.uk/cals/calsres/

SECOND LANGUAGE READING AND INCIDENTAL VOCABULARY LEARNING

Rob Waring and Paul Nation

ABSTRACT

This article reviews the current state of knowledge regarding the relationship between second language reading and incidental vocabulary acquisition. The review shows that the picture we have built up over the years of incidental vocabulary acquisition is less clear then we once thought. Recent research shows that our previous data does not fully show how well vocabulary is retained after reading, nor how the type of test used to gather learning data can be dramatically affected by the type of test used. The paper concludes with some implications for pedagogy and future research.

Introduction

The notion that we could learn a lot, or most, of our vocabulary through reading, or more particularly comprehensible written input, is now entrenched within second and foreign language teaching. This paper will review what we know about the relationship between reading in a foreign language and vocabulary acquisition. We shall then look at the implications for teaching and research.

What do we know about the relationship between vocabulary and reading in second languages?

In recent years we have learned a lot about the relationship between vocabulary learning and reading. For example, we have learned something about how many words we need to know in order to read effectively in a foreign language; the rate of vocabulary uptake and decay from reading; the number of meetings it takes to learn a word; and the retention of recently learned words. We will review each of these in turn.

The most striking examples of the positive effects of extensive reading come from the 'Book Flood' studies (Elley, 1991). These involved spending a large proportion of the English programme on extensive reading where learners chose from a wide range of interesting texts. The Fiji book flood study (Elley and Mangubhai, 1981) lasted eight months and brought about dramatic improvements in a wide range of language skills including reading comprehension, knowledge of grammatical structures, word recognition, oral repetition, and writing. Unfortunately, this study did not include a measure of vocabulary growth, but it is clear that the improvement on the various measures used could not have occurred without substantial vocabulary growth. Elley (1991: 378-379) saw the success of the book flood being due to five factors.

1   Extensive input of meaningful print.
2   Incidental learning.
3   The integration of oral and written activity.
4   Focus on meaning rather than form.
5   High intrinsic motivation.

It is likely that these same factors will be important in an extensive reading programme with vocabulary learning goals.

What coverage rate is needed to be able to read pleasurably?

Laufer (1989) and Liu and Nation (1985) have shown that unless there is at least 95% or higher coverage rate (the percentage of the vocabulary that is known by the reader) of the running words in a text, the probability of successful guessing of unknown words will be severely reduced. Hu and Nation (2001) suggest it should be at least 98%. This was determined by using several texts with different unknown word rates and by measuring adequate comprehension. No subject reported adequate comprehension of text with only 80% coverage rate, but at 90% and 95% coverage a few did, and only at the 98% level did most subjects gain adequate comprehension. Carver (1994) suggests a similar figure of 98-99% for native speakers for reading to be pleasurable. Coverage rate and vocabulary size are closely related and so we will now look at how large a vocabulary is needed to reach these high coverage rates.

How many words do we need to know in order to read effectively in a foreign language?

Most studies in this area have looked at the learning of English but some have looked at other languages (e.g. Ostyn and Godin 1985 looked at Dutch). Laufer (1992) has suggested that a vocabulary of 3000 word families of general English is enough for a good understanding of a general English text such as a novel. Other estimates have been as high as 5000 word families (Hirsh and Nation 1992) as an adequate level for pleasure reading.

The number of words needed for the reading of technical texts such as science texts, or newspapers is larger than for less formal texts. There are several reasons for this. Firstly, there are higher proportions of academic and technical words in formal informative writing. Chung and Nation (2003) found that 38% of the running words in an anatomy text and 17% of the words in an applied linguistics text were technical words. Some of these words were drawn from the high frequency and academic vocabulary, but more were from what would in other texts be considered low frequency words. Secondly, because of the heavy cognitive demands of formal texts, a higher text coverage is likely to be needed. Where the text content is important we are less tolerant of unknown words. Thirdly, if formal reading is for academic purposes, then several subject areas and topics are likely to be covered. The more diverse the range of subjects and topics, the much larger the vocabulary required (Sutarsyah, Nation and Kennedy 1994).

In an extensive reading programme for elementary and intermediate foreign or second language learners, graded readers need to play an important role (Day and Bamford 1998; Hill 1997). This is because the various levels of graded readers provide ideal vocabulary coverage conditions for a range of levels of achievement within the elementary and intermediate levels. These readers cover the 300 to 3000 word vocabulary range. Because graded readers are controlled or simplified material, some teachers and researchers feel that they are not adequate models for language learners. This is a mistaken view because readers can only process text fluently at or near their own ability level. If a text contains too many unknown words, the reader must process the text intensively and slowly which changes the reading into a study activity rather than a fluency building one. Thus, without graded readers, elementary and intermediate learners would not be able to do extensive reading at the proper vocabulary levels (Nation and Deweerdt 2001) and a very important means of reading skill development, language consolidation and vocabulary learning would not be available to them. Corpus research on the conditions for vocabulary learning provided by graded readers (Nation and Wang 1999) provides useful guidelines on how to use such readers and suggests that the levels of some of the many graded reading schemes could be usefully redesigned. In spite of these minor shortcomings, graded readers provide an enormously helpful resource for the development of reading skills, vocabulary growth and other associated benefits for language learners.

At what rate can learners learn new words from their reading?

The most basic question is whether learners can learn from reading at all. Clearly they can, as the millions of learners who have learned English from text books and natural reading can attest. The common-sense notion that we can learn new words from reading has led some to suggest that conducting research to determine if learners can learn from their reading is rather futile. Meara (1997) suggests this is like putting seeds in a pot only to confirm that they will grow into flowers.

While he is undoubtedly right that it will only confirm the obvious, this kind of research is important because it impacts on the pedagogical aspects of language learning and teaching. This type of research will help us understand the rate of uptake of new vocabulary, and how this affects the amount of reading that needs to be done. Moreover, it can provide us with data to determine the likelihood of a word being learnt and thus help us determine the appropriate balance of known versus unknown words in texts so that we can maximize the likelihood of uptake. Secondly, it provides us with data that can assist us in comparisons with data from other vocabulary

Table 1. A representative sample of often cited studies of vocabulary growth from reading in a foreign language (adapted from Waring and Takaki 2003)

Study	Population	Exposure	Materials read	Type of test used	Vocabulary gains
Pitts, White and Krashen (1989) Experiment 1	35 ESL learners	6700 words	2 chapters of Clockwork Orange with 123 nadsat words	Multiple-choice test	6.4%
Pitts, White and Krashen (1989) Experiment 2	16 ESL learners	6700 words	2 chapters of Clockwork Orange plus 2 scenes of the video	Multiple-choice	8.1%
Day, Omura and Hiramatsu (1991)	92 High school EFL learners and 200 university EFL learners	1032 words	Short story	Multiple-choice	5.8%
Dupuy and Krashen (1993)	42 ESL learners	15 page of text	French text plus watched a video	Multiple-choice	25% of the words the controls did not know
Hulstijn (1992)	65 EFL learners	907 words	Advertisement in Dutch	State the meaning of 12 words	17.6%
Horst, Cobb and Meara (1998)	34 EFL learners	21,232 words	Simplified version of novel, The Mayor of Casterbridge	Multiple-choice and a word association test	20.0% of the MC test items and 16% of the word associations
Zahar, Cobb and Spada (1999)	144 ESL	2383 words	Short novel The Golden Fleece		7.8%

learning methods to find ways of combining effective methods of teaching and learning for a given goal. For example, from a vocabulary learning perspective we can see where reading can best benefit the learner and where it does not. We can determine whether it is better to just read a text to pick up the vocabulary, or learn the vocabulary from text first before reading. Thirdly, these data can also help us predict what the learners will be able to learn in a given time and with a given effort, which has implications for curriculum, syllabus and lesson design.

There have been quite a number of studies which have looked at how much vocabulary is learned from reading in a foreign language. Representative examples include, Day, Omura and Hiramatsu (1991); Dupuy and Krashen (1993); Grabe and Stoller (1997); Horst, Cobb and Meara (1998); Mason and Krashen (1997) and Pitts, White and Krashen, (1989) among a long list of others. Table 1 has a sample of some of the more commonly cited research that has looked at the amount of vocabulary learned from reading in a foreign language.

The general picture from these studies shows that learners do learn vocabulary from their reading, which is of course both encouraging and to be expected. On average, the returns are somewhat low. It seems that of the items tested about one tenth of the target words will be learned. These data, of course, do not cover any other words that were met in the texts that were not tested.

One of the most striking things about Table 1 is that the results differ quite widely. We have rates as high as 25% and as low as 5,8%. What are the reasons for this? Part of the answer lies in the words that were tested. If a word was met only once, there is a much less likelihood that it would be learned compared to one that had been met often. Obviously not all the words in the studies were met the same number of times and each study could have had a different ratio of frequently met items compared to the number of items met only once.

Moreover, some of the words would have been concrete and thus easier to learn whereas others were more abstract and probably harder to learn. Whether a word has been learned or not depends a lot on what one considers learning to be, and defining the 'learning' of a word is no easy task. For example, we can broadly assume that there are two levels, or stages, of word learning. The form-meaning relationship is the first of these which involves matching the spelling of a word with its meaning. The second one refers to the additional knowledge of a word that a learner will need in order to have full command of it. This 'deeper' knowledge may include its inflections and derivations, the shades of meanings of the word, its collocations or colligations, and the knowledge of its restrictions of use, whether it is formal or informal, pejorative or not, its frequency of use, whether it is more common in speech or written text and so on.

Another part of the answer related to this is the type of test used. Not all the tests used in these studies were of the same type. Research trying to ascertain the rate new vocabulary is learned from reading must be answered in specific terms. It is clearly very difficult to ascertain the level of knowledge of all aspects of word knowledge and so typically vocabulary gains from reading are assessed by form-meaning type tests such as multiple-choice or translation tests that assess only the first level of word knowledge. While this is certainly of value, it understates the importance of other types of word knowledge and possibly overstates the importance of the form-meaning relationship type of word learning when conducting incidental reading research.

Data from Waring and Takaki (2003) suggest that the type of test used can greatly affect the results one will obtain. A variety of measures are needed including what are called sensitive tests (Nation, 2001: 358-361). Waring and Takaki used three types of test to see if there were any major differences. The first test was a simple sight recognition test ('Have you seen this word in the text, yes or no') where meaning was not needed to answer the question. The second test was a standard multiple-choice test of the words with the three distractors from different semantic fields. The third test was a translation test whereby the target word was required to be translated into the L1 (receptive recall of the meaning).

Their results show clearly that the type of test can greatly affect the amount of words considered to be learned. The sight recognition test produced the higher scores (15.3 of the 25 target words (61%) were recognized), the multiple choice test the next highest (10.6/25 or 42.4%) and then the translation test the lowest (4.6/25 or 18.4%) on the immediate post test. Using several tests presents a fuller picture of learning and in future work of this kind it will be important to collect data from more than one type of test so that we can better understand what is going on when learners read.

A third reason for the variations between learning uptake rates would be differences in the rate at which learners are able to take on board new information from the texts used in the experiments. If a text had been inordinately difficult (for example where the coverage rate was too low), it would have made the working out of the meaning of unknown words, and the comprehension of the text, that much harder.

Waring and Takaki's (2003) figures show that incidental vocabulary learning from reading is occurring at several levels. Their translation test is the most demanding test requiring unassisted recall of a word meaning. This is clearly a desirable state of knowledge, but the incidental learning of vocabulary is best considered as a cumulative process where learners build up knowledge of a word through repeated encounters over a reasonable period of time. Thus being able to choose an appropriate meaning from a list of plausible choices as in the multiple-choice test shows that at least some knowledge of form and meaning has been retained even though in many cases it may not be enough for unassisted recall. Further meetings will strengthen this knowledge. Similarly, the ability to recognize which words occurred in the text and which did not indicates that some familiarity with the form of a word has been achieved. This is an important step in vocabulary learning and there is some evidence that learning to accurately recognise the form of a word is quite a substantial undertaking. Once a form is familiar, working out what it means is the next obvious step.

Thus in research on incidental learning from reading, the use of several tests is necessary to gain a more accurate and balanced picture of learning. There is no one best way to test learning. Each test reveals another facet of information about the kinds of learning that can take place.

The number of times we need to meet a word to learn it from reading
Guessing a word from context and remembering it are two different things. In studies of incidental vocabulary learning, it is thus important to see what conditions help learning. The subjects in the Saragi, Nation and Meister (1978) study learned 93% of the words that had been presented to them six times or more but words presented to learners fewer than six times were learned only by half their subjects. Jenkins, Stein and Wysocki (1984) discovered that only about 25% of their learners had learned a word after 10 meetings. Nagy, Herman and Anderson (1985) showed that the likelihood that a word would be learned after one meeting was 0.15. Swanborn and Glopper (1999) in a meta-analysis of 20 incidental learning experiments in L1 generalized that the chances of an unknown word being learned were also about 15%. In other words, only one in seven of the target words were likely to be learned in one meeting. In a replication experiment, however, Herman, Anderson, Pearson and Nagy (1987) only found a rate of .05 (1 in 20) for authentic texts. Rott (1999) also concluded that six encounters was an adequate number. Other studies (Waring and Takaki 2003) have shown the value of higher repetition rates. Zahar, Cobb and Spada (2001) found that weaker learners needed more encounters to learn a word than more proficient learners. This seems to fit the maxim that the more you know, the easier it is to learn. The exact rate of this would need to be identified empirically as well.

How well is the learning retained?

One aspect of this incidental learning which is not often examined is how well the words are retained over time. Such data can provide us with insights into how fragile the learning is and thus reflect real life situations more accurately. Nation and Wang (1999) in a corpus study of graded readers calculated that in order for learners to gain enough repetitions to ensure secure learning, they would have to read at least one graded reader every week.

The Waring and Takaki (2003) experiment used 15 subjects to examine how many words of varying frequencies of occurrence rates were learned and retained from the reading of one graded reader – *A Little Princess*. Through an analysis of the target text they identified 25 target items of varying frequency levels (from those occurring 15 to 18 times to those appearing only once). The spelling of each word was changed to resemble an imaginary nonce word to ensure that each test item was unknown. Three test types were administered over three testing periods – immediate post test, one month later and three months later.

An analysis of the rate of learning depending on the frequency of occurrence showed that words that had been met more frequently were more likely to be learned and were more resistant to decay. The average scores after three months dropped from 61% to 33.6% on the form recognition test, from 42.4% to 24.4% on the multiple choice test and from 18.4% to 3.6% on the translation test. The data suggest that, on average, the meaning of only one of the 25 items on the translation test will be remembered after three months (or about a 4% uptake). A deeper analysis of the scores shows that the meaning of none of the items that were met fewer than eight times will be remembered three months later as measured by the translation test. The biggest drop was on the translation test that assessed unprompted recall. This suggests that the word meaning knowledge decays faster than that of simple word form recognition.

This research thus questions the data already presented above on the rate of uptake as no retention data are given to illuminate the decay rates. These findings have direct implications also for the number of times it takes to learn a word. Above we stated that it was about between 6 to10 meetings, but none of this research had decay data. An extrapolation from the findings in Waring and Takaki suggests that these should be considerably raised to account for knowledge decay. This figure might need to be raised to 20 meetings or more if we take retention beyond the immediate post test as our criterion for learning. Clearly, from a pedagogical point of view, this implies that an effective reading programme which has included vocabulary learning as one of its goals, must provide for repeated encounters with the same words over reasonably short time periods.

Implications

The findings on coverage, repetition, and decay have direct implications for language teaching and learning. These implications will be broken into two groups – those affecting pedagogy, and those affecting research issues.

Implications for pedagogy

One implication from the above is that readers must be exposed to text that is accessible if they wish to read and learn with ease. There is clearly a threshold at which learners are able to take advantage of being exposed to text. This was hinted at in several pieces of research (e.g. Laufer-Dvorkin, 1991; Lai, 1993). If the text is too difficult then little learning can take place – especially if the known coverage rate is lower than 98%. Moreover, the 'guessing from context' research also suggests that unless the reading is done at a high level of vocabulary coverage, little learning will take place.

The data here also confirm the need to provide materials at the right instructional levels both for intensive and extensive reading. The rate of uptake data seem to confirm Nation's contention (2001: 150) that there are three levels of instruction regarding the coverage rate of known versus unknown words. Nation suggests that the appropriate text coverage level for intensive reading (i.e. involving the direct learning of new language features) can be less than 95%. However, for extensive reading with the aim of language growth, the rate should be between 95-98%. For extensive reading for fluency improvement it should be 99-100%.

Moreover, if the aim of the reading task is to increase language knowledge, imposing a text on learners of different ability levels for the purpose of pleasure reading is likely to lead to frustration on the part of some learners. This is because some learners will be able to easily handle the text and get something from it, while others will be swamped with new language and learn nothing. If the text is too difficult, the weaker subjects will not be able to guess successfully and the advanced ones will be limited by knowing most of the words anyway and thus will meet fewer unknown words and structures. Thus an extensive reading program of learner self-selected reading where learners read at their own comfortable reading rate with material at an appropriate level is important for incidental vocabulary learning. An effective extensive reading programme needs to engage the learners to get their sustained attention, needs to encourage large quantities of reading to get adequate vocabulary repetition, and needs to provide texts at the right coverage levels to allow unknown vocabulary to be adequately dealt with.

Even with this adjustment to current knowledge, does this imply that reading is the best way to learn vocabulary? A number of researchers suggest that reading is the key. Stephen Krashen is probably the most famous proponent of the need for reading and especially Sustained Silent Reading, Pleasure Reading and Extensive Reading. Krashen has stated that:

> Reading is good for you. The research supports a stronger conclusion, however. Reading is the only way, the only way we become good readers, develop a good writing style, an adequate vocabulary, advanced grammar, and the only way we become good spellers.
>
> (Krashen 1993:23)

There is no doubt that reading a lot can contribute to our reading ability, our writing style and can help build our vocabulary and aid our spelling. No one would suggest that the *only* thing one should do to be good at a foreign language would be to read. However, Krashen comes close to saying this. Krashen's claim suggests that reading is a very effective way of building up a lot of one's language competence. But his claim goes further than that. It suggests that all other methods of vocabulary learning are less effective, or less useful than simply just reading. While few people voice such an extreme view, there are numerous others who support the notion that 'simply reading' is an extremely beneficial way of learning vocabulary.

How true is this? In order to find out, we need to look beyond only reading to master an 'adequate vocabulary' (presumably Krashen is referring to receptive recognition vocabulary only), and look closely at other methods of vocabulary learning to see how effective they are. Hulstijn (1988) investigated the amount of vocabulary learned from reading only versus reading plus additional vocabulary activities. His study concluded that reading should be supplemented by other activities. Zahar, Cobb and Spada (1999) concur suggesting that intentional learning should supplement the reading as it is a more effective way of learning words. All studies comparing incidental with intentional learning show that intentional learning is more efficient and effective. This should not be seen as a competition between incidental and intentional learning. Rather, a well balanced language programme should make good use of both types of learning. One without the other is inadequate.

Most research data we have looked at suggest that learners will learn about 3-6 words per hour of reading. If we assume that a student in school has 3-4 hours of exposure to English each week for 40 weeks a year, and one third of that is reading, this totals about 50 hours of reading per year, or vocabulary growth of between 150 to 300 words per year, not counting natural forgetting from the reading alone. Of course different programs will have different learning rates and these figures would have to be amended as such. Clearly then a program heavily emphasizing an input heavy approach would have to demonstrate considerable gains to be a valid main strategy. Learners would benefit from some combination of direct intentional study to build a larger vocabulary. This would have to be accompanied by adequate reading at the right level and in the right amounts to consolidate and enrich the vocabulary learned from direct learning.

Implications for research
We hope that more researchers will adopt a multi-test format in future research to provide a richer picture of the types of word knowledge that learners can gain. For example, it would be instructive to see how well learners can pick up a word's spelling, its collocations, its derivatives and so on. Similar research also needs to be done on the rate of acquisition of multi-word units. Moreover, we hope that these researchers will also obtain decay data to provide a clearer picture of the actual learning that has taken place.

Recent research on incidental vocabulary learning through extensive reading has shown that it can be a major source of learning, providing it is part of a substantial and sustained reading programme. Vocabulary learning is also helped by the direct learning and teaching of vocabulary, by the need to use vocabulary in speaking and writing, and by opportunities to become fluent with vocabulary across the skills of listening, speaking, reading and writing. It is thus important to see incidental vocabulary learning through extensive reading in this wider context. The important question is not 'Which way of learning vocabulary is the best?', but 'How can the various ways of learning vocabulary be used to help each other and provide optimal vocabulary growth?'. Incidental vocabulary learning through reading is an important and effective part of this balance. The very informative recent research and descriptions of good practice have provided useful guidelines for setting up reading programmes to help this learning. The present major challenge is to get teachers to put these guidelines into practice.

References

Arnaud, P.J.L. and Béjoint, H. (1992) *Vocabulary and Applied Linguistics*, Macmillan: London.

Carver, R.P. (1994) 'Percentage of Unknown Vocabulary Words in Text as a Function of the Relative Difficulty of the Text: Implications for Instruction', *Journal of Reading Behavior*, **26**, 4, 413-437.

Chung, T. and Nation, I.S.P. (2003) 'Technical Vocabulary in Specialised Texts', *Reading in a Foreign Language*, **15**, 2, 103-116, http://nflrc.hawaii.edu/rfl.

Day, R.R. and Bamford, J. (1998) *Extensive Reading in the Second Language Classroom*, Cambridge University Press: Cambridge.

Day, R. R., Omura, C., and Hiramatsu, M. (1991) 'Incidental EFL Vocabulary Learning and Reading', *Reading in a Foreign Language*, **7**, 2, 541-551.

Dupuy, B. and Krashen, S.D. (1993) 'Incidental Vocabulary Acquisition in French as a Foreign Language', *Applied Language Learning*, **4**, 1 and 2, 55-63.

Elley, W. B. (1991) 'Acquiring Literacy in a Second Language: the Effect of Book-Based Programs', *Language Learning*, **41**, 3, 375-411.

Elley, W. B. and Mangubhai, F. (1981a) *The Impact of a Book Flood in Fiji Primary Schools*, NZCER: Wellington.

Elley, W. B. and Mangubhai, F. (1981b) 'The Long-term Effects of a Book Flood on Children's Language Growth', *Directions*, **7**, 15-24.

Grabe, W. and Stoller, F. (1997) 'Reading and Vocabulary Development in a Second Language: a Case Study', in Coady and Huckin, *Second Language Vocabulary Acquisition*, 98-122, Cambridge University Press: Cambridge.

Herman, P.A., Anderson, R.C., Pearson, P.D., Nagy, W.E. (1987) 'Incidental Acquisition of Word Meaning from Expositions with Varied Text Features', *Reading Research Quarterly* **22**, 3, 263-284.

Hill, D.R. (1997) 'Survey Review: Graded Readers', *ELT Journal*, **51**, 1, 57-81.

Hirsh, D. and Nation, P. (1992) 'What Vocabulary Size is Needed to Read Unsimplified Texts for Pleasure?', *Reading in a Foreign Language*, **8**, 2, 689-696.

Horst, M., Cobb, T., and Meara, P. (1998) 'Beyond a Clockwork Orange: Acquiring Second Language Vocabulary through Reading', *Reading in a Foreign Language*, **11**, 2, 207-223.

Hsueh-chao, M.H. and Nation, I.S.P. (2001) 'Unknown Vocabulary Density and Reading Comprehension', *Reading in a Foreign Language*, **13**, 1, 403-430.

Hulstijn, J.H. (1992) 'Retention of Inferred and Given Word Meanings: Experiments in Incidental Vocabulary Learning', in P. Arnaud and H. Bejoint, 113-125.

Hulstijn, J.H. (1988) 'Experiments with Semi-Artificial Input in Second Language Acquisition Research', in B. Hammarberg (ed.) *Language Learning and Learner Language*, **8**, 28-40. Papers from a Conference held in Stockholm and Åbo 17-18 October, 1988. Scandinavian Working Papers on Bilingualism (issued from the Centre for Research on Bilingualism: University of Stockholm).

Jenkins, J.R., Stein, M.L. and Wysocki, K. (1984) 'Learning Vocabulary through Reading', *American Educational Research Journal,* **21,** 4, 767-787.

Krashen, S. (1993) *The Power of Reading. Insights from the Research,* Englewood, Co.: Libraries Unlimited.

Lai, F. (1993) 'The Effect of a Summer Reading Course on Reading and Writing Skills', *System,* **21,** 1, 87-100.

Laufer, B. (1992) 'How much Lexis is Necessary for Reading Comprehension?', in P. Arnaud and H. Bejoint, 126-132.

Laufer, B. (1989) 'What Percentage of Text-Lexis is Essential for Comprehension?', in C. Lauren and M. Nordman (eds.) *Special Language: From Humans Thinking to Thinking Machines,* Multilingual Matters: Clevedon.

Laufer-Dvorkin, B. (1991) *Similar Lexical Forms in Interlanguage,* Gunter Narr Verlag Tübingen: Tübingen.

Liu Na and Nation, I.S.P. (1985) 'Factors Affecting Guessing Vocabulary in Context', *RELC Journal,* **16,** 1, 33-42.

Mason, B. and Krashen, S. (1997) 'Extensive Reading in English as a Foreign Language', *System,* **25,** 1, 91-102.

Meara, P. (1997) 'Towards a New Approach to Modelling Vocabulary Acquisition', in Schmitt and McCarthy, 109-121.

Nagy, W. E., Herman, P., and Anderson, R. C. (1985) 'Learning Words from Context', *Reading Research Quarterly,* **20,** 233-253.

Nation, I.S.P. (2001) *Learning Vocabulary in Another Language,* Cambridge University Press: Cambridge.

Nation, I.S.P. and Deweerdt, J. (2001) 'A Defence of Simplification', *Prospect,* **16,** 3, 55-67.

Nation, P. and Wang, K. (1999) 'Graded Readers and Vocabulary', *Reading in a Foreign Language,* **12,** 2, 355-380.

Ostyn, P. and Godin, P. (1985) 'RALEX: an Alternative Approach to Language Teaching', *Modern Language Journal,* **69,** 4, 346-355.

Pitts, M., White, H., and Krashen, S. (1989) 'Acquiring Second Language Vocabulary through Reading: a Replication of the Clockwork Orange Study Using Second Language Acquirers', *Reading in a Foreign Language,* **5,** 2, 271-275.

Rott, S. (1999) 'The Effect of Exposure Frequency on Intermediate Language Learners' Incidental Vocabulary Acquisition through Reading', *Studies in Second Language Acquisition,* **21,** 1, 589-619.

Saragi, T., Nation, I. S. P., and Meister, G. F. (1978) 'Vocabulary Learning and Reading', *System,* **6,** 2, 72-78.

Schmitt, N. and McCarthy, M. (eds) (1997) *Vocabulary: Description, Acquisition and Pedagogy,* Cambridge University Press: Cambridge.

Sutarsyah, C., Nation, P. and Kennedy, G. (1994) 'How Useful is EAP Vocabulary for ESP? A Corpus Based Study', *RELC Journal,* **25,** 2, 34-50.

Swanborn, M.S.L. and de Glopper, K. (1999) 'Incidental Word Learning while

Reading: a Meta-Analysis', *Review of Educational Research,* **69,** 3, 261-285.

Waring, R. and Takaki, M. (2003) 'At What Rate Do Learners Learn and Retain New Vocabulary from Reading a Graded Reader?', *Reading in a Foreign Language,* **15,** 2, 130-163.

Zahar, R., Cobb, T. and Spada, N. (2001) 'Acquiring Vocabulary through Reading: Effects of Frequency and Contextual richness', *Canadian Modern Language Review,* **57,** 3, 541-572.

LEXICAL INFERENCING PROCESSES IN L1 AND L2: SAME OR DIFFERENT?

Focus on Issues in Design and Method

Kirsten Haastrup, Dorte Albrechtsen, and Birgit Henriksen

ABSTRACT

This article deals with lexical inferencing processes drawing on a study of Danish learners of English. An important objective of this study is to compare the same informants' lexical inferencing processes in their mother tongue Danish and their first foreign language English. In order to address this issue parallel inferencing tasks in the two languages were developed. Focus in the article is on methodological issues in design such as task development and on illustrating how introspective methods in the form of verbal protocols are used.

Introduction

This study deals with the way in which informants try to guess the meaning of unfamiliar words, and the lexical inferencing processes that are elicited by giving informants the task of inferring the meaning of a word placed in a context that is comprehensible to them. Since the cover term 'word guessing strategies' includes several different approaches, one of which is contextual guessing, we shall start by presenting our own more comprehensive definition of lexical inferencing (Haastrup 1991:13).

> The process of lexical inferencing involves making informed guesses as to the meaning of a word in the light of all available linguistic cues in combination with the learner's general knowledge of the world, her awareness of the co-text and her relevant linguistic knowledge.

The research literature includes a number of studies of lexical inferencing in the informants' native and foreign language, as well as studies of advanced and intermediate learners (Haastrup and Henriksen, forthcoming).[1] However, no study has so far, to our knowledge, been made of the same informants' completion of inferencing tasks in both L1 and L2, and therefore one important objective of the present study is to do just that. This means that our Danish informants will be required to engage in inferencing tasks in both Danish (their L1) and English (L2, their first foreign language).

The article reports on work in relation to an ongoing project *Processes in writing and vocabulary acquisition in English as a foreign language*.[2] The overall aim of this project is to trace the development and possible interactions of processes in writing, lexical inferencing as well as various aspects of vocabulary knowledge in learners of a foreign language at three educational levels in a within-subjects design. This development is also investigated in relation to the learners' processing ability and knowledge of vocabulary in their mother tongue. The focus of this paper is exclusively on the lexical inferencing part of the project, and we shall only consider data from two of our informant groups: grade 7 pupils (aged 13-14) and first year university students of English.

In the first section of the paper, dealing with design, special emphasis will be given to task development. In order to address the research question concerning lexical inferencing approaches in informants' L1 and L2, it is necessary to have two elicitation tasks that, as far as possible, run in parallel. In pursuit of this aim, significant decisions have to be made about not only the choice of *texts* but also the selection of *test words*. A major issue in the second section, which deals with method, is the analysis of verbal protocols. The lexical inferencing process is studied through a concurrent think-aloud procedure followed by retrospection. At an early point in the discussion, illustrative examples of protocol analysis are provided in order to give some idea of what kind of data are under consideration. In addition, the examples serve the purpose of highlighting similarities and differences between the same informants' approaches to lexical inferencing in their first and second languages. As an introduction to the discussion of preliminary results, a brief outline will be given of the analytic framework behind the protocol analysis. The paper is rounded off with a section headed 'Perspectives'.

Issues in Design

The tasks: Texts and test words

Two parallel tasks were devised, one in Danish and the other in English, the description below being based primarily on the latter. The task consisted of five short factual *texts*, all dealing with different topics. We sought subject matter that was likely to be of interest to as many informants as possible and which was not too cognitively demanding. In this regard, we focussed chiefly on the youngest group, namely the 13-year olds in Grade 7, bringing in areas such as popular science and anthropology, through, for example, texts on great explorers. The ideal was that the context in which the test words were embedded should be fully comprehensible to all informants. This was obviously a difficult requirement to meet since the informant group spanned such a wide range; consequently glosses were provided to certain significant words in the text (although obviously not to the test words themselves).

Illustration of the matching of topics in three texts.

	Danish text	English text
Explorers	Columbus and America	Robert Scott and the South Pole
Health	Body and movement	Health in a developing country
Animals	Dinosaurs	Apes and monkeys

Thirty *test words* were included in the task, the aim being to find items that would be unknown to all the participants. Although this constraint naturally had to apply to all those taking part, it was felt that the higher level group, namely the university students, were crucial in this regard. If it was considered that a word would be unknown to them, then it was most improbable that it would be known to the lower level seventh graders.

In the selection of the test words, a second criterion was essential, namely that there had to be items representative of three main word types:
• words with no linguistic cues to meaning (e.g. *serendipity*)
• words with potential cues to meaning in the form of affixes (e.g. *recalcitrant*)
• words that have more than one linguistic cue to meaning: a core portion plus a prefix and/or a suffix (e.g. *abysmal*).

The above categorisation into word types was based on previous linguistic analysis combined with evidence from field testing of the test words on Danish informants with near-native English proficiency. It is essential to have all the different word types represented, since (as will be explained below) they are expected to elicit different forms of processing. The task contains an equal number (i.e. ten) of test words representing each of the three types.

It came as no surprise to discover that it was extremely difficult to find Danish words likely to be unknown to the higher group, since university students should in principle be expected to have an extensive vocabulary in their mother tongue. Moreover, items that were over-technical would look out of place in texts on general topics, the more so given that we had adapted the texts to make them more easily intelligible to the 13-year old informants. Many of the 30 Danish test words that were found through extensive field testing were either items of some antiquity (although still in use) or alternatively loanwords derived from other languages (most often Latin).

Examples of test words from both languages

	Danish	English
Words without linguistic cues	bulle	squalor
Words with linguistic cues	akvatiske	sustenance
	aerofobi	undergirding

By way of illustration, short extracts from two texts (one in each language) are provided below.

English (extract from text about the explorer Scott and his men on their journey to the South Pole)
> ... they were hit by another storm that lasted for days. With quiet **fortitude** they waited for death in the tent. Later, in the year 1912, other explorers found the tent and the frozen bodies, as well as Scott's diaries and **copious** notes with much information.

Danish (extract from text about Columbus)
> Dommene over ham har vekslet lige fra den rene forgudelse, der vil søge ham **kanoniseret**, til den rene fornægtelse af en hvilken som helst god egenskab. Når det gælder Columbus' bidrag til videnskaben om søvæsen, fandt han ganske vist magnetnålens **deklination**, men i øvrigt blev han overgået af mange af sine samtidige.

Procedure
- **Pre-test**

The informants completed a pre-test immediately before being given the actual inferencing task so as to discover which items were familiar to participants from the university group; these words could then be excluded from the analysis. At this stage, the test words were presented in alphabetical order, out of context and in isolation. Time allowed for completion of this component of the task was four minutes.

- **The lexical inferencing task with concurrent think-aloud**

The informants were then given the actual inferencing task with the 30 test words embedded in running text. For each test word (printed in bold face) they were instructed to verbalise all their thoughts and ideas, ending their considerations with the following phrase (original in Danish) 'So I think that the word means ...' Time allowed: 32 minutes.

- **The retrospective task**

The informants were then presented with the same inferencing text, but with a slightly different lay-out. This time they were required to concentrate on 20 of the test words, and they were instructed to focus on what had helped them to arrive at their suggestion for word meaning in the task just completed. So for each test word they had to end their verbalisations with the phrase, 'What helped me arrive at my suggestion for word meaning was...'. Time allowed: 20 minutes.

In summary: with reference to task design, the Danish and the English inferencing tasks were exact parallels with respect to types of topics, types of test words and procedures.

Issues related to method: focus on protocol analysis

From tape-recording to protocol analysis
In transcription from spoken to written language, and especially in any subsequent translation, informant texts lose much of their authenticity. It is particularly difficult to translate portions in which the informant uses cues from a Danish word. If such use of L1 cues is to be made obvious in the English version the results generally read oddly. Consequently, where in the following section learner texts have been quoted, the original untranslated version has been given for the benefit of readers with a knowledge of Danish.

What information are we seeking?
This section is intended to give the reader a general impression of the data and to illustrate the kind of analyses undertaken in the study. In essence, we are seeking answers to questions involving three aspects of the lexical inferencing process:

• Which knowledge sources do the informants activate? The answer to this question is one or more of the following: (1) contextual cues (2) intralingual cues and (3) interlingual cues.

• Do informants make use of the activated cues by combining or even integrating them into their suggestions for word meaning?

• Do they arrive at a suggestion for word meaning and if so, is it an accurate guess, a reasonable guess that makes sense in thecontext or a wild guess?

In the comments to the protocol analyses below, we shall use the terms 'top cues' and 'bottom cues', terms borrowed from comprehension research (top-down and bottom-up processes). Refer to Figure 1 below.

```
Top cues  ⎡ context
          ⎣ semantics

          ⎡ collocation
          │ syntax
          │ word class
          │ lexis
          │ morphology
Bottom cues ⎣ orthography/phonology
```

Figure 1. Hierarchy of cue levels

When informants activate cues from context and/or engage in meaning considerations inspired by a linguistic cue from the test word, this is referred to as use of top cues. In contrast, when they pay exclusive attention to, for instance, orthographic similarity between the test word and another word without signalling any apparent concern for meaning, this is an example of the use of bottom cues. When informants use approaches that are likely to lead to an accurate or reasonable guess, the term 'potentially effective processing' will be employed.

We shall firstly consider examples from the protocols of one of our seventh grade informants, and then secondly from a university informant. The protocol examples have been selected to illustrate trends found in the analysis of protocols from a small sub-set of informants from the extreme ends of the population. The procedure used below is to begin each example by quoting from the transcribed and translated protocols for a particular test word, and subsequently append analysis and commentary.

Interpreting protocols from a Grade 7 informant

In this section we shall examine examples from a Grade 7 informant whom we shall call Alice. The first three examples from her L2 inferencing will be followed by examples from her L1 inferencing. For both languages the protocol examples are selected to illustrate approaches to the different word types. We have attempted to show the informants' pronunciation of words in orthographic form. Think-aloud is referred to as TA and retrospection as Re. Text within <xxx> refers to the informant's reading aloud from the printed text.

L2 inferencing

1. Test word *fortitude* in context: '...the men were hit by another storm that lasted for days. With quiet **fortitude** they waited for death in the tent.'

Extract from protocols
[The informant pronounces the word *fortitude* approximately as 'fourtide'. Her mispronunciation of the English word makes her think of the Danish word *fortid* ('past').]

		Original	Translation
Fortitude	TA	"fourtide" <with quiet "fourtide"> "fourtide" – så tror jeg det betyder "fortid"	"fourtide" <with quiet "fourtide"> "fourtide" – I think the word means "past"
	Re	Original ...så det var "fourtide" – så så tænkte jeg på det danske ord *fortid* – "fourtide" – det var det – det var hvad jeg sagde – jeg kunne se der var et andet dansk ord der mindede om det	Translation ...so this was "fourtide" – then then I thought of the Danish word *fortid* – that was it – that was what I said – I could see that there was another Danish word which resembled it

Here Alice activates an L1 cue triggered by similarity between the way she reads and especially pronounces the test word *fortitude* and the Danish word *fortid*. This is evident from the retrospection stage where she states in direct terms 'there was another Danish word which was like it'. Thus the informant appears to be focussed on the test word at the levels of orthography/phonology, and there is no indication that she considers to what extent her suggestion for word meaning makes sense in the context.

2. Test word *dissemination* in context: 'Today scientists are working on the undergirding of theories about the South Pole area as well as on the **dissemination** of knowledge.'

Extract from protocols

		Original	Translation
Dissemination	TA	"desimæsjen" – *legitimation* [udtalt på dansk med tryk på sidste stavelse]	"decimation" – *legitimation* [pronounced as a Danish word with stress on the final syllable]
	Re	Original Og så "desimæsjen" – "mæsjen" – der kendte jeg *information* [udtalt på engelsk] – det er "information" [udtalt på dansk med tryk på sidste stavelse] – og så var det "mæsjen" der hjalp mig	Translation And then "decimation" – "-mation" – there I knew *information* [pronounced as the English word] – that is "information" [pronounced as the Danish word with stress on the final syllable] – and then it was "-mation" that helped me

The extracts above reveal many of the same phenomena as in the first example. Once again we can see Alice paying attention exclusively to formal similarity without concerning herself with whether this is accompanied by semantic similarity, i.e. meaning relatedness. However, whereas the first protocol from this informant showed us that Alice used formal similarity between the test word and an L1 word, it is clear from the present protocol that the informant activates both an intralingual cue, i.e. *information* (English pronunciation) and a Danish one (*information* – Danish pronunciation). According to the informant herself (in the retrospection component), it was the '-mation' part of the test word that inspired her to look for items including this particular string of sounds.

3. Test word *squalor* in context: 'In the poor world people are killed by the conditions they live under, the **squalor** and the lack of food and money.'

Extract from protocols

		Original	Translation
Squalor	TA	<...the "skwælow" and the lack of food and money> – "skwælow" – det ved jeg bare ikke – "skwærelow" ... eller – "skwærelåre" – *square dance* (latter) så jeg ved ikke hvad ordet betyder	<...the "squailow" and the lack of food and money> – "squailow" – I just don't know – "squarelow" – ... or – "squarelore" – *square dance* (laughs) – so I don't know what the word means
	Re	No retrospection	No retrospection

The third example serves to underline the informant's concern with similarity between the English words *squalor* and *square*. Alice attempts to pronounce the test word in a variety of ways which gradually sound more like *square*, eventually triggering *square dance*. All activated cues clearly originate from the orthographic/phonological level. In our experience, when informants use expressions such as 'this looks like' or 'this sounds like', it is very often accompanied by embarrassed laughter, which is possibly a sign that the informant at heart doubts the validity of bottom cues. Even though this informant does not actually use expressions of this type, there is a clear parallel. Moreover, in the present TA transcript, there are overt statements of disbelief; Alice herself says that she does not consider 'square dance' a likely meaning for this word.

In summary, one may conclude that all three examples show Alice's use of cues from the bottom level of the cue hierarchy – an approach which has very little chance of leading to an accurate estimate of word meaning. We shall now turn to examples derived from Alice's Danish inferencing task.

L1 Inferencing

Examples have been selected to illustrate that when Alice is working in her native language she introduces strategies that are potentially more effective than those she employed in the L2 task. Nevertheless, her L1 protocols also include several instances of ineffective approaches.

1. Test word *akvatiske* ('aquatic') in context (text on dinosaurs): 'Endelig er

der fiskeøglerne, som er **akvatiske** krybdyr, hvis kroppe gjorde dem perfekt tilpassede til at fange hurtigtsvømmende bytte.' ['Finally there are the ictosaura which are aquatic reptiles whose bodies made them perfectly adapted to catch fast swimming prey.']

Extract from protocols
[The informant mispronounces the Danish word, consistently putting stress on the third syllable rather than the second.]

	TA	Original	Translation
Akvatiske		"Akva'tiske" <endelig er der fiskeøglerne som er "akva'tiske" krybdyr> – ak- (latter) det skulle være noget som *akvarium* – "akva- tiske" [udtalt med kort pause mellem *akva* og *tiske*] – det er nok noget med at de er sure – eller sådan nogen krybdyr de – farlige krybdyr – jeg tror det betyder farlige	"Akva'tiske" [reads aloud from Danish text] – ak- (laughter) – it should be something like *aquarium* [Danish word for fish tank] – "akva- tiske" [pronounced with a short break between *akva* and *tiske*] – it probably means that they are cross – or reptiles like that are – dangerous reptiles – I think it means dangerous
	Re	Original "Akva'tiske" den den kunne jeg ikke helt finde ud af men jeg tænkte på akvarium – og *tiske* – det det ved jeg ikke helt om hvad jeg gjorde – det var et svært ord – jeg tænkte i hvert fald på akvarium	Translation "Akva'tiske" this one this I couldn't quite work out but I thought of *akvarium* [Danish word for fish tank] – and *tiske* – I don't quite know what I did – it was a difficult word – I definitely thought of *akvarium*

In the TA protocol, Alice activates a linguistic cue, namely the Danish word *akvarium*. She also makes an attempt at word analysis, dividing the test word into *akva* ['aqua-'] and *tiske* ['-tic'], with -*tiske* carrying the main stress. However, the retrospection procedure supports the idea that her actual suggestion for word meaning does not stem from these cues; rather it seems likely that the suggestion 'farlige' ('dangerous') is based on activation of contextual cues, notably her knowledge of the world (in this instance of dinosaurs): 'or reptiles like that are – dangerous reptiles – I think it means dangerous'. We note that new features in Alice's inferencing in her L1, as compared with L2, are her activation of contextual cues and also her attempts at word analysis.

2. Test word *ensvarme* [literally 'same heat'] in context (text on dinosaurs): 'Men vi ved ikke om dinosaurerne var **ensvarme** eller vekselvarme.' ['But we don't know whether dinosaurs were warm-blooded or cold-blooded.']

Extract from protocols

	TA	Original	Translation
Ensvarme	TA	...jeg tror ordet betyder – ensvarme altså ens – det er noget med hvis man nu er tvillinger så er man jo ens så (suk) så jeg tror at det er noget med at dinosaurerne var ens og så varme – ensvarme eller vekselvarme	....I think the word means – same heat [Danish ensvarme] – that is 'same' – it is just as with twins then you are the same so (sigh) so it's probably that dinosaurs were the same and hot – warm-blooded (*ensvarme*) or cold-blooded (*vekselvarme*)
	Re	...at dinosaurerne var ensvarme – måske at de havde den samme varme indeni sig tror jeg jeg tænkte på – eller sådan noget	...the dinosaurs were warm-blooded – perhaps that they had the same heat inside them – that's what I believe I was thinking of – or something like that

The test word *ensvarme* ('warm-blooded') is a compound made up of two Danish high-frequency words in simple juxtaposition – *ens* meaning 'same' and *varme* meaning 'heat'. It is therefore predictable that the informant would know the meaning of both components and is able to integrate the two cues to meaning. In the TA she says about *ens*: 'it is just as with twins then you are the same'. And at the retrospection stage she adds: '*perhaps that they had the same heat inside them* – that's what I believe I was thinking of'. The portion italicised in the previous section may be considered to be Alice's suggestion for word meaning in the form of a paraphrase. In our analysis, we would consider this accurate guess to be the result of the use of linguistic cues to meaning, supported by the activation of cues from the co-text stemming from *ensvarme* being juxtaposed with *vekselvarme* (cold-blooded).

3. Test word *vankundige* (English: 'ignorant') in context: 'Mange almindelige mennesker synes, at dinosaurer er spændende at læse om, men i forhold til eksperterne er vi naturligvis **vankundige**.' [Many ordinary people think that it's interesting to read about dinosaurs, but compared with experts, we are naturally ignorant']

Extract from protocol

	TA	Original	Translation
Vankundige	TA	...det er nok noget med at de at de er naturligt bekymrede eller – de er naturlige – de er som de fleste mennesker ville være hvis der var dinosaurer i området – det tror jeg det betyder	....I think it has to do with them being – they are naturally concerned or – they are natural – they are as most people would be if there were dinosaurs in the area – this is what it means I think
	Re	*No retrospection*	*No retrospection*

Our interpretation of this is that Alice's suggestion for word meaning 'naturligt bekymrede' (they are worried, which is a natural reaction in the situation) is arrived at through cues from the co-text (*naturligvis* occuring close to the test word) and the use of knowledge of the world (clearly most people would worry if they thought dinosaurs were in the neighbourhood).

Interpreting protocols from a university informant

The examples quoted below have been selected to illustrate *similarities* in the way in which an informant from the university group (we shall call him Niels) approaches lexical inferencing tasks in English and Danish. The focus is on similarities, as opposed to differences, for this group because a clear pattern of this kind has been observed in data gathered from university level informants. Let us now consider the manner in which Niels deals with a Danish and an English test word of the same word type: Danish *aerofobi* and English *undergirding*. Both items are classified as words containing linguistic cues to meaning.

L1 Inferencing

1. Test word *aerofobi* in context: 'I nogle tilfælde er valget let; hvis man for eksempel lider af **aerofobi**, ved man i hvert fald, hvad man skal vælge fra.' ['In some cases the choice is easy; if, for instance, you suffer from aerophobia, you definitely know what not to choose.']

Extract from protocols

	TA	Original	Translation
Aerofobi	TA	...så skal man nok ikke ud at flyve i svævefly – jeg tror ordet betyder flyveskræk – *aero* det må være noget med luft – det må være noget med at befinde sig i luften	....in that case it's not a good idea to go gliding – I think the word means fear of flying – *aero* must be something with air – it must be something with being in the air
	Re	Original	Translation
		Aero betyder luft og fobi betyder en sygelig frygt for eller en stærk ubegrundet frygt – i hvert fald må det være frygten for luft eller at være i luft – som højdeskræk så kunne være...	*Aero* is air and phobia is a a – an abnormal fear of or a strong unfounded fear – anyway it must be fear of air or of being in the air – such as fear of heights

In the TA protocol, the informant Niels infers from the context that 'it's not a good idea to go gliding'. Niels suggests that the word means 'fear of flying', adding that *aero* must be something with air. He thus activates a linguistic cue from the first part of the compound, *aero-* and, by paraphrasing it in Danish, indicates that he is concerned with meaning, so operating at a semantic level. From the retrospection protocol, it is evident that Niels also uses the second part of the compound, *fobi*, which he correctly paraphrases as 'abnormal fear'. By using information from the TA and the Retro in tandem, we can infer that Niels cannot quite make up his mind as to whether *aerfobi* means 'fear of flying in the air' or 'fear of the air'. However, there can be no doubt that he has understood the main sense of *aerofobi*, namely 'fear of air', and he has arrived at his suggestions for word meaning by letting cues from context interact with linguistic cues to meaning.

L2 inferencing

1. Test word *undergirding* in context: 'Today, scientists are working on the **undergirding** of theories about the South Pole area...'

Extract from protocols (in TA informant verbalises in English)

Undergirding	TA	*Original* ...undergird is to support – or to find something that can support and in this example a theory – a gird is a is erm a beam a headbeam for example something that braces erm something something that supports it makes it stronger	
	Re	*Original* Det er at understøtte - altså det de arbejder på – ting der kan understøtte teorierne – det passer også med at – *gird* - det er sådan forstærkende – understøt – ja understøttende er nok det eneste ord jeg lige kan...	*Translation* This means to support – that is what they are working on things that can support the theories – that fits in with *gird* too – this is like strengthening – support – suppporting is probably the only word I can think of

In the TA protocol, Niels starts out by using a cue from the co-text, quickly establishing that in this particular context it is a theory that is to be supported. He then finds a word stem *gird*, which *he* relates to 'beam', and the last part of his utterance centres round the idea of 'supporting'. This approach is resumed in the retrospection section by the statement 'this means to support'. Niels goes on to test whether his suggestion would fit the context: 'that is they are working on things that can support the theories' and immediately follows up with a self-reassurance that 'this fits in with *gird* too'.

Comparison of lexical inferencing approaches in English L2 and Danish L1

For the **seventh grader Alice** we can summarise our observations in the following way. Faced with an *L2 task* with long, strange-looking foreign test words, Alice seems hypnotised by whatever similarity she can find between something in the test word and a familiar feature from an L2 or an L1 word. It does not seem to worry her that such similarities occur at microlevel, for instance, merely a short sequence as when <squa> in 'squalor' makes her think of 'square dance'. Moreover, the idea of 'sound alike' or 'look alike' is not accompanied by considerations of meaning relationships – this becomes all too clear when suggestions for meaning are simply wild guesses, indicating that there has been no attempt to check if the suggested words fit the context.

In the *L1 task*, on the other hand, we see Alice using different strategies – she actually employs some quite effective approaches along with the less effective ones. For instance, it is noteworthy that she activates contextual cues, both in the form of co-text cues and her own knowledge of the world. In trying to spot linguistic cues to meaning, she makes attempts at word analysis and finds, for instance, the word 'akvarium' (in relation to the test word 'akvatisk').This means that she has moved beyond the orthographic/ phonological level of 'sound alike/ look alike' up to the lexical level through citing an authentic Danish word.

One may tentatively conclude from this that in the case of this *seventh grader informant*, there is a clear *difference* between the lexical inferencing she employs for the L2 task as opposed to the L1 task. In both cases, the informant uses ineffective approaches, but in the L1 she shows an additional use of potentially more effective processing.

A comparison of how the **university student** deals with words such as 'aerofobi' and 'undergirding' in the lexical inferencing tasks in L1 and L2 leads one to conclude that in both cases a *similar approach* is employed. **Niels** activates contextual cues as well as linguistic cues to meaning and integrates these. He thus demonstrates use of effective processing in both languages, as will be elaborated below.

Aspects of the analytic framework

In the previous section, our aim was to provide the reader with a general impression of the kind of data we work with, and give some idea of what information we are seeking. In our comments above on the extracts from the protocols, we have tried to avoid excessive use of specific terminology since it is beyond the scope of a short article such as this to account for the taxonomies through which the protocols have been analysed. Note that the major framework of the first taxonomy (hierarchy of cue levels) was outlined in Figure 1, and we shall now proceed to a brief overview of what we regard as the most important types of processing. For a full explanation of the elaborate comprehensive analytic framework and its theoretical base, see Haastrup (1991).

The protocol extracts have been used to provide illustrations of three processing types termed: (1) pure top processing, (2) top-ruled interactive processing and (3) bottom-ruled processing. Let us now consider each of these in turn.

The most basic type of processing is called *pure top processing* because it involves the use of contextual cues only. Although simple, it is the potentially most effective processing system for test words without linguistic cues to meaning such as the word 'squalor'.

For words with linguistic cues to meaning, the potentially most effective processing is *top-ruled interactive processing*. Here informants make use of what cues they can find in the test word itself, and then proceed to consider meaning; they will either be certain that suggestions for word meaning do actually fit the context, or will remember explicitly to check that this is indeed the case. Thus the term 'interactive' implies that more than one cue level is involved, while 'top' reflects the fact that processing is directed from the top.

But, as can be seen from the seventh grader examples, we also find *bottom-ruled processing*, where informants seem preoccupied with formal similarity between the test word and, for instance, another Danish word. This means that they proceed no further than the activation of bottom cues; at least their verbalisation includes no sign of them questioning whether formal similarity is accompanied by meaning relatedness. This is called bottom-ruled processing and recalls the well-known phenomena of 'false friends' and 'deceptive similarity'.

Before proceeding to a discussion of preliminary results, it is necessary to explain a few more terms:

Potentially effective processing refers to pure top processing and top-ruled interactive processing. It is called 'potentially effective' because its effectiveness depends on additional factors, notably the informant's declarative word knowledge. In contrast, bottom-ruled processing generally proves to be ineffective processing.

The concept of *adaptability* is related to words with linguistic cues to meaning. The hallmark of adaptability is the extent to which informants distinguish between words with linguistic cues to meaning (for instance *dissemination*), and words lacking such cues (for instance *squalor*), and adapt their processing accordingly.

Inferencing success is measured in the following manner. A scoring system is applied where a precise guess receives two points, a partially correct guess one point, while a wrong or missing guess scores zero. Points for each of the 30 items are added up to a total score for the 30 test words, giving a potential maximum score of 60 points.

Discussion of preliminary results

The preliminary results discussed below should be regarded more as tendencies that have been observed during the ongoing analysis work rather than final results. Figures presented in the tables are based on a small sub-set of the total informant population, four informants from the university group (including Niels) and five from the Grade 7 group (including Alice). Means have been calculated for each of the two groups.

Table 1. Percentages of processing
Mean percentages for each group: The percentages are based on the number of valid items. The

	Percentages of processing			
	Potentially effective processing		Adaptability	
Language	L1	L2	L1	L2
University group (n=4)	98	98	54	34
Grade 7 group (n=5)	69	57	18	4

number of valid items vary. Mean number of valid items: Potentially effective processing: University group: Danish: 28 English: 27. Grade 7 group: Danish: 20 English: 16. Adaptability: University group: Danish: 18 English: 18. Grade 7 group: Danish: 12 English: 10.

For the **university group**, the patterns that emerge are that use of *potentially effective processing* shows up with exactly the same high score (98 percent) for both the first and the second language tasks. Adaptability, however, comes out as superior in the L1 as compared to the L2. In the case of the **Grade 7 students**, this group performs better for both measures in the L1 than in the L2. For potentially effective processing the difference is not so great. However, when it comes to adaptability, the gap between L1 and L2 processing widens, giving 18 percent versus 4 percent. In summary, the overall impression for this group is one of difference, and extrapolating from this preliminary analysis, we expect to find, once we have analysed the data *in toto*, significant differences for all three measures, but most notably for adaptability.

It is possible to make the following tentative interpretation based on these observations. Which resources can a typical **university student** draw on? They will have developed many of the necessary prerequisites for effective processing in both the L1 and L2. These will include procedural skills (such as reading and word analysis skills), in addition to extensive linguistic knowledge – notably of vocabulary. However, for vocabulary knowledge there is probably a difference. Vocabulary knowledge – both in terms of size and organisation – will clearly be superior in the L1 as compared with the L2.

The typical **seventh grader student** will lack many of the resources that the university students have at their disposal. What is left for them to draw on? We can expect that even though their reading in the L2 is far from fluent and they lack knowledge of the world, they may have some luck with pure top processing, especially in the cases where cues from the co-text are strong. For words with linguistic cues to meaning, such as for instance *dissemination*, their L2 vocabulary is far too restricted for them to arrive at accurate guesses.

Let us try to relate this for the two groups to the results for *adaptability* in Table 1. For both groups, scores drop considerably from L1 to L2 and it is necessary to ask why this should be. The answer seems to be that the complex processing required for a word like 'dissemination' presupposes extensive vocabulary knowledge, and such knowledge includes vocabulary size, i.e. declarative knowledge of lexical items and knowledge of affixes, in addition to procedural skills in the form of word analysis skills. This may explain why for the parameters where vocabulary knowledge plays a major role, i.e. *adaptability* and *success*, we find overall much poorer performance for the L2 than for the L1 – and why the gap is wider in the case of the Grade 7 group.

For *inferencing success* we find the following mean scores (maximum score 60): for L1 inferencing the university group has a mean of 37 and the Grade 7 group a mean of 6; for L2 inferencing the former group has a mean of 27 and the latter of 1. Thus for this sub-set of informants there is – as expected – a great difference between the two groups with respect to both languages, the extreme case being the mean score of 1 for L2 inferencing in the Grade 7 group.

Rounding off, we may state the following. To the question raised in the title of this article, namely whether processing in the L1 and the L2 is the same or different, the answer seems to be that this all depends on the informant group. Our university informants show great similarity in their processing in the two languages, even though their guesses are less accurate for L2 than for L1. For the seventh graders, there are substantial differences between their performance in the two languages, and performance is always better in the first than in the second language. If we focus on the adaptability, one must conclude that in relation to L1, the university students clearly outperform the Grade 7 group. However, when it comes to the L2, there is a clear drop, not only for the seventh graders but also for the university group, but also here they outperform Grade 7.

Perspectives

We want to conclude by reiterating what we believe are essential features of the design of our study, not only for the informant groups, but also for the tasks they are required to perform. Firstly, the three informant groups take in a wide range of both age and language proficiency; this is certainly an asset in terms of the validity of the study, but, as we have stated earlier, it creates definite design problems. Secondly, with regard to the elicitation tasks, we have seen that the choice of test words is of crucial significance.

The adaptability figures (see Table 1 above) serve to emphasise how important it is to include different word types, and to investigate this aspect systematically. In the past, this has not always been given due consideration. Finally, we need to specify the research perspective, namely the extent to which focus should be on the process *vis-à-vis* the outcome of the process. We have found it extremely valuable for our analyses to cover both the process and the product perspectives.

An essential matter that must be taken into account is the language factor, more specifically the distance (or perceived distance) between the L1 and L2. When the final results of this study are eventually presented, it will be necessary to bear in mind that these data are derived from English and Danish – two closely related languages and cultures. Language typology is bound to play a significant role, especially as far as word types are concerned, and to the processing types with integration of linguistic cues to meaning. A consequence of this is that there must be limitations as to the generalisations that can be made. Nevertheless, in this regard it is encouraging to discover that a lexical inferencing study has been conducted for Ilokano (a Philippine language) by Soria (2001), in which the author has successfully adopted criteria set by Haastrup (1991) for the choice of word types.

We have illustrated some of the ways in which we are going to explore the full data material with focus on the two parallel sets of data – one in L1 and one in L2 – from the same informants. We have examined data from the extreme ends of our informant range and pointed to significant patterns emerging so far. Once data from our Grade 10 informants have been encoded, we expect this information to form an intermediary link between Grade 7 and university level informants, which should help us understand how lexical inferencing develops in the two languages. For instance, when our Grade 7 informant Alice reaches Grade 10 we expect to see that much of her ineffective bottom-ruled processing in L2 inferencing will be substituted by the more effective processing types she introduced in her L1 inferencing already in Grade 7.

Another of the research issues on our agenda is the relationship between lexical inferencing and reading skills and vocabulary size. Lexical inferencing is closely related to text inferencing, in other words to reading comprehension. L2 reading research is still struggling with the question of whether good L2 reading is a matter of reading skills or L2 proficiency – both aspects doubtless play a role, but we do not yet know what the balance is between the two. The same goes for lexical inferencing. We would reiterate that it is to be expected that crucial factors contributing to effective lexical inferencing in both L1 and L2 are reading skills, word analysis skills and vocabulary knowledge. We therefore expect much explanatory power to come out of our data on tests in L1 and L2 vocabulary size and from tests on reading comprehension. This issue is taken up in another contribution to the present volume (Henriksen, Albrechtsen & Haastrup).

Notes

[1] This article includes a meta-analysis of the studies from the 1990s referred to in the references.
[2] The authors gratefully acknowledge financial support from the Danish National Research Council for the Humanities (Statens Humanistiske Forskningsråd) in the form of a 3-year research grant, which has made this study possible.

References

Haastrup, K. (1987) 'Using Thinking Aloud and Retrospection to Uncover Learners' Lexical Inferencing Procedures', in Færch, C. and G. Kasper (eds.), *Introspection in Second Language Research*, 197-212, Multilingual Matters: Clevedon.

Haastrup, K. (1991) *Lexical Inferencing Procedures or Talking about Words*, Gunter Narr Verlag: Tübingen.

Haastrup, K. and Henriksen, B. (forthcoming) 'Lexical Inferencing Studied in Relation to Comprehension and Vocabulary Acquisition'.

Huckin, T. and Bloch, J. (1993) 'Strategies for Inferring Word Meanings from Context: A Cognitive Model', in Huckin, T., Haynes, M. and J. Coady, J. (eds.), *Second Language Reading and Vocabulary*, 153-176, Ablex Publishing Corporation: Norwood, New Jersey.

Lawson, M. J. and Hogben, D. (1996) 'The Vocabulary-Learning Strategies of Foreign-Language Students', *Language Learning*, **46**, 1, 101-135.

Mondria, J.A. and Wit-de Boer, M. (1991) 'The Effects of Contextual Richness on the Guessability and the Retention of Words in a Foreign Language', *Applied Linguistics*, **12**, 249-267.

Paribakht, S. and Wesche, M. (1999) 'Reading and "Incidental" L2 Vocabulary Acquisition. An Introspective Study of Lexical Inferencing', *Studies in Second Language Acquisition*, Special Issue on 'Incidental L2 Vocabulary Acquisition: Theory, Current Research and Instructional Implications', **21**, 2, 195-224.

Rott, S. and Williams, J. (2003) 'Making Form-Meaning Connections while Reading: A Qualitative Analysis of Word Processing', *Reading in a Foreign language*, **15**, 1.

Soria, J. (2001) 'A Study of Ilokano Learners' Lexical Inferencing Procedures Through Think-aloud', *Second Language Studies*, **19**, 2, 77-110.

THE RELATIONSHIP BETWEEN VOCABULARY SIZE AND READING COMPREHENSION IN THE L2

BIRGIT HENRIKSEN, DORTE ALBRECHTSEN AND KIRSTEN HAASTRUP

ABSTRACT

This article explores the relationship between foreign language learners' L2 vocabulary size and their L2 reading comprehension scores on the basis of data from two groups of Danish learners of English (Grade 10 pupils and university students). Vocabulary and reading tests were administered in both L2 and L1. A high correlation between L2 vocabulary and reading scores is observed, confirming previous research findings that L2 vocabulary size is a strong predictor of L2 reading skills. In line with earlier findings, the results show that only learners with high L2 reading scores managed to do well on the reading test, whereas learners with small vocabularies, as predicted, had difficulties with L2 reading. The findings, however, also suggest that *a probability zone* can be defined, within which not only vocabulary size but other variables, such as lexical inferencing skills and the organisational structure of the lexicon, which determine reading ability, must be considered.

Introduction

As discussed by Waring and Nation (this volume), a strong relationship exists between vocabulary size and reading – one which is clearly complex and not unidirectional (Hsueh-chao and Nation 2000; Nation 2001). Most of our vocabulary acquisition takes place incidentally through reading, and a substantial knowledge and understanding of the vocabulary included in written texts is needed in order to read any text type effortlessly and with success. Laufer (1992, 1997) focused on the role of lexical knowledge in reading comprehension, suggesting that we must have immediate and automatic access to at least 3000 word families (i.e. around 5000 lexical items) in any given language to ensure good reading comprehension. Qian and Schedl (2004:28) have also argued that many researchers 'view vocabulary knowledge as a major direct factor in reading comprehension.'

Nobody would question that there is a need for a reasonable level of L2 language-specific knowledge in the form of vocabulary, grammar and discourse knowledge, in addition to sufficient background knowledge, in order to achieve good text comprehension. On the other hand, it is natural to assume that learners who have the benefit of having effective reading skills in their first language can utilize this underlying general reading ability when trying to read in a second or foreign language. In other words, a strong correlation is to be expected between L1 and L2 reading skills. In a large empirical study of Dutch learners' reading comprehension and vocabulary knowledge in both L1 and L2, Schoonen et al. (1998) found that for older learners above a certain L2 level substantial metacognitive knowledge of reading was an important predictor of reading comprehension results. For younger learners, however, the study showed that L2 vocabulary knowledge turned out to be a more significant predictor of L2 reading ability.

Laufer (1997) refers to a number of second language studies which have discovered a strong positive correlation between L2 learners' reading scores and their vocabulary test scores, showing that L2 vocabulary size clearly proves to be a very good predictor of L2 reading comprehension. The correlation between reading and vocabulary has been found to be much stronger than, for example, between reading and syntactic knowledge (Laufer 1997). As confirmed by a number of researchers, lack of sufficient L2 vocabulary knowledge 'short-circuits' the transfer of effective reading strategies (Clark 1980; Schoonen et al. 1998), a point indeed highlighted in the sub-title of Clark's article 'when language competence interferes with reading performance'. As stressed by Lee (1997), efficient use of background knowledge (schemata) can compensate for lack of linguistic knowledge, but 'to rely on a small set of knowledge sources without complete linguistic knowledge may lead a reader to construct inaccurate meaning...'. In other words, a certain level of L2 linguistic knowledge, especially lexical knowledge, is needed to ensure good L2 reading comprehension

In this paper, we will look more closely at the relationship between L2 vocabulary size and L2 reading comprehension, using data from our current study of Danish learners' acquisition of English as a foreign language. On the basis of the previous research findings discussed above, the general expectation would be that a strong correlation exists between the size of our informants' L2 vocabulary and their reading scores in the L2. As discussed by Hsueh-chao and Nation (2000) and Nation (2001:144), we can define the threshold vocabulary needed for reading comprehension in many ways, either as an 'all-or-nothing' phenomenon or as a probabilistic boundary. In other words, would we want to say that, for a learner who has not crossed the boundary of for example the 5000 words estimated by researchers, good L2 reading comprehension is not at all possible? Or is a weaker version of this view more likely, according to which it is not impossible, but highly improbable, that a learner below a certain vocabulary level will be able to achieve adequate understanding on an L2 reading task? This question will be addressed in relation to a discussion of whether it is possible to pinpoint the L2 vocabulary level needed for the specific L2 reading test given to our informants.

The study

The Danish research project

The data we report on here has been taken from the Danish research project (*Processes in writing and vocabulary acquisition in English as a foreign language*) which has been funded by the Danish National Research Council for the Humanities.[1] The overall aim of the project is to investigate the relationship between knowledge and skills in the foreign language (English) and the mother tongue (Danish) from the same informants, both over time (longitudinally) and across three learner groups (cross-sectionally). Cross-sectional data from Time 1 was collected from 30 informants from each of the following levels of education: grade 7 (pupils aged 13-14), grade 10 (pupils aged 16-17) and from first year university students of English (mean age 20). Time 2 data is being collected in the spring of 2004. For the project, a range of tasks in both English (L2) and Danish (L1) is being used: two different types of writing task; inferencing tasks, in which the informants are required when reading to guess the meaning of unknown words; three different lexical network tasks, and vocabulary and reading tests.

By collecting data across such a wide range of tasks, it is hoped to set up complex profiles of our informants' abilities spanning these different research areas across the two languages, making it feasible to explore possible relations in the various skills and knowledge areas investigated. The focus in this paper is exclusively on the reading and vocabulary tests included in the task battery. (For a discussion of some of the Danish writing and lexical inferencing data, see the two articles in this volume by the same author team).

The informants

In this paper, we shall consider only the results from the reading and vocabulary tests from the tenth graders (30 informants) and first year university students (30 informants) who participated in our data collection at Time 1. Because of the generally lower proficiency level of our Grade 7 informants, both in L2 and L1, these participants were not given the same reading tests as the informants from the higher educational levels but were given other more grade-appropriate reading tasks. The information from their data therefore would lend itself only to intra-group comparisons across tasks and will not be discussed here. The two older groups were, however, presented with the same L2 and L1 reading and vocabulary tests, so a direct comparison both between tasks and across groups is indeed possible.

The vocabulary tests
It was decided to use Paul Nation's 'Levels Test' as a test of L2 (English) vocabulary (see Nation 2001: 416-424). The version chosen was the updated form of Nation's Vocabulary Levels Test, developed by Schmitt, Schmitt and Clapham. This test has the advantage of being well described; it has been validated (see Schmitt, Schmitt and Clapham 2001); and has often been used as a general measure of vocabulary size in vocabulary acquisition research and in a range of pedagogical studies. As Meara (1996:38) has pointed out, the Levels Test is 'the nearest thing we have to a standard test of vocabulary'. Another advantage of the test format is that it scrutinizes vocabulary across a number of vocabulary frequency bands, so it is well suited to informant groups like ours which span large age and proficiency ranges. However, the Academic Word Level includes academic words across a range of different frequency bands, and consequently it was decided to leave this word level out of the final version employed for our test purposes. The final test which was used included 120 test items across four frequency bands (2000, 3000, 5000 and 10,000 word level).

Only a few Danish standardized vocabulary tests exist, and so unfortunately it was not possible for us to find an existing Danish vocabulary test, comparable with the Levels Test, which would fit our research purposes. A parallel L1 vocabulary test was therefore devised specifically for the project by ourselves in collaboration with Anja Knudsen (one of our MA students). The validation of the task was carried out in close collaboration with Dr Norbert Schmitt of the University of Nottingham, who had validated the original L2 version of the Levels Test.[2] The L1 task follows the original L2 test format as closely as possible, with 120 test items across four frequency bands. However, because it had been developed to measure the size of our informants' native language, and with the purpose of being suitable for discriminating across native speakers from our three age groups, it was decided to choose four frequency levels which included more low-frequency items than Nation's L2 test. A direct comparison between the scores obtained on the two tasks is consequently impossible: the Danish L1 version, because it includes more low-frequency vocabulary items, is comparatively more difficult than the L2 test. This procedure was necessary in order to make the test challenging enough for both the tenth graders and the university students.

The reading tests

As a test of L2 reading, we decided to use the Nelson Denny Reading test, a test designed to test the reading skills of both L1 readers and L2 learners of English. This test includes seven different reading texts, each representing different text genres and topics. A multiple-choice format is employed in which those taking the test are required to choose between five possible answers for each comprehension question; maximum score is 38 and time on task is 32 minutes. The benefits of using this test format is that it is widely used, has been validated and standardized,

When looking for a parallel L1 reading test, it was our hope also to be able to find a test which had been standardized, and which was as far as possible comparable to the format of the Nelson Denny test. Once again, very few Danish reading tests are available for the grade levels appropriate to this project. We eventually settled upon an L1 reading test developed by Elisabeth Arnbak and Carsten Elbro (Centre for Reading Research, University of Copenhagen)[3]. This test includes three different text types, representing different genres and topics; a multiple-choice format is used, in which those taking the test must choose between four possible answers to each comprehension question; maximum score is 35 and time on task is 40 minutes. The benefit of using this test format is that it is comparable with that of the Nelson Denny Test, has been standardized, and was developed for testing the reading skills of Danish L1 readers.

More than 30 informants from each educational level initially participated in the Time 1 data collection procedure. The results of the Danish reading test were used as an objective selection criterion when the final 30 informants from each educational level were selected for analysis and this enabled us to ensure that both low-level and high-level participants were included in the study. Since the results of the L1 reading were used in our screening procedure, the discussion in this paper will primarily focus on the L2 results.

Results

General results

A comparison of the scores on the tests across our two informant groups (see Table 1) reveals, as might be expected, that our university students in general did better than the tenth graders across all four tests.[4] This difference across the two groups is apparent no matter whether we compare the informants on the group mean scores, the range of scores, or the number of informants who fall below or above the mean score for all 60 participants. It should, however, be noted that some of the more gifted Grade 10 informants performed better on all the tasks than some of the weaker university students.

Even if the L1 vocabulary test does include more low-frequency vocabulary items than the L2 test, it is in no way strange that the L1 vocabulary scores are higher.

Table 1. Comparison between L1 and L2 vocabulary and reading tests across groups

Tests	General Mean	No. of informants below or above general mean		Group results		
Vocabulary size L2 (MS: 120)	82.5	10th g.	Below: 22	10th g.	Group Mean: 70.9 Score range: 28 Ö 110	SD: 20.86
			Above: 8			
		Univ.	Below: 6	Univ.	Group Mean: 94.1 Score range: 67 Ö 118	SD: 14.95
			Above: 24			
Reading L2 (MS: 38)	25.7	10th g.	Below: 19	10th g.	Group Mean: 22.2 Score range: 7 Ö 36	SD: 7.38
			Above: 11			
		Univ.	Below: 7	Univ.	Group Mean: 29.2 Score range: 16 Ö 37	SD: 6.45
			Above: 23			
Vocabulary size L1 (MS: 120)	92.5	10th g.	Below: 19	10th g.	Group Mean: 83 Score range: 43- 111	SD: 18.60
			Above: 11			
		Univ.	Below: 6	Univ.	Group Mean: 102 Score range: 85 Ö 120	SD: 9.80
			Above: 24			
Reading L1 (MS: 35)	19.7	10th g.	Below: 15	10th g.	Group Mean: 18.5 Score range: 7 Ö 32	SD: 6.91
			Above: 15			
		Univ.	Below: 9	Univ.	Group Mean: 20.8 Score range: 11 Ö 29	SD: 4.84
			Above: 21			

The L2 vocabulary and reading tests

As had been predicted, a high correlation was found between the scores on the L2 vocabulary size test and the L2 reading test for both informant groups (Grade 10: r = .85 (p< 0.05); university: r = .79 (p< 0.05)). This is confirmed if we examine more closely the results from the L2 tests. Twenty-four out of the 28 participants from the two groups who scored *below* the general mean score for all 60 informants on the L2 vocabulary test also scored below the general mean on the L2 reading test, and thirty out of the 32 informants whose scores on the L2 vocabulary test were *above* the general mean also achieved scores above the general mean on the L2 reading test. These results confirm the expectations from the research literature, namely, that a close relationship between vocabulary and reading assessment exists, i.e. that vocabulary size in the foreign language is a strong predictor of reading comprehension in the L2. If we look more closely at the 24 informants with scores *below average* on both the L2 vocabulary and L2 reading test, 17 of these also gained *below average* scores on the Danish reading test. In other words, their low reading scores on the L2 reading test may be caused by a combination of a small vocabulary in the L2 and poor reading skills in the L1.

Seven of the informants with below average scores on the L2 reading test (see Table 2 below), gained scores on the L1 reading test above the general mean. In other words, these informants seem to be slightly above average or even fairly good readers in the L1, but not in the L2. A closer look at their scores on the L2 vocabulary may give us a clue to why they failed to do as well on the L2 reading test as one might have predicted from their L1 reading test. All of them obtained below average L2 vocabulary scores, so for these learners, a small vocabulary seemingly 'short-circuits' the possible transfer of well-developed reading skills from the first language; a result in line with the research literature outlined in the introduction.

Table 2. Informants with below average scores on both L2 tests, but with above average scores on the L1 reading test

Tests	Mean	Inf. 1	Inf. 2	Inf. 3	Inf. 4	Inf. 5	Inf. 6	Inf. 7
Vocabulary L2	82.5	49	55	62	65	68	75	77
Reading L2	25.7	18	22	17	19	19	16	22
Reading L1	19.7	24	26	24	27	22	23	23

As predicted, a strong correspondence was found between L2 vocabulary and L2 reading for a majority of the 60 informants from both educational levels, i.e. most learners with low scores on the vocabulary test also gained low scores on the reading test and most learners with high vocabulary scores also obtained high reading scores.

Four informants, however, clearly go against this general pattern (see Table 3 below), i.e. the relationship between the results on the two L2 tests are much more confusing and difficult to explain. Informant 8 gained above average vocabulary scores in both languages, but failed to do well on any of the reading tests. Apparently, this learner has not developed good reading skills and was therefore unable to use his above average vocabulary size in both languages to support him sufficiently in the reading process in either of the languages tested.

Table 3. Informants that go against the general tendency

Informants	L2 vocabulary (mean: 82.5)	L2 reading (mean: 25.7)	L1 vocabulary (mean 92.5)	L1 reading (mean 19.7)
Uni - 8	88	18	102	14
Grade 10 - 9	74	32	91	23
Grade 10 - 10	72	26	88	24
Grade 10 - 11	71	29	91	23

More interestingly, three tenth graders (informants 9, 10, and 11) managed to do better than expected on the L2 reading test in view of their fairly low scores on the L2 vocabulary test. All other informants with similar or even higher vocabulary scores obtained, as predicted, reading scores below average. The three informants under scrutiny are, however, also above average readers in their first language, so it looks as if they have been able, in spite of a small L2 vocabulary, to transfer good reading skills from their L1 to their L2. Analysis of their lexical inferencing skills and lexical network structure may reveal whether any of these aspects can add to our understanding of their ability to do so well within their group on the reading tests (L2 group mean: 22.2// L1 group mean 18.5). Phrased differently, do these participant have a well-structured network that gives them more immediate access to related lexical items in the reading process, and which may help them to obtain a better global understanding of the texts they read? And are they able to apply complex and appropriate lexical inferencing strategies to aid the comprehension of unknown words when reading? These points will be taken up below.

Can we pinpoint the L2 vocabulary level needed for doing well on the L2 reading test?

The results seem to mirror the findings from the research literature, confirming the close relationship between L2 vocabulary size and L2 reading. Up till now, we have discussed only the size of vocabulary needed to understand the majority of words in a text, and to apply good reading strategies in more general terms. In the research literature, the exact vocabulary size for being above the vocabulary threshold has been roughly estimated at figures ranging from 3000 to 5000 words (Laufer 1997). It is worth considering whether, on the basis of the results obtained from the L2 vocabulary and reading tests from our two groups, one can estimate more precisely which scores on the Nation's Levels Test correspond with either high or low L2 reading scores. Moreover, a closer look at the scores may give us more information as to why some of our informants seem to go against the expected general tendency found in the data.

None of the 15 informants with a vocabulary score *below* 70 on the L2 vocabulary test achieved an L2 reading score above the general mean. Moreover, all 23 informants with a vocabulary score *above* 90 performed well on the L2 reading task. For the 22 informants with vocabulary scores *between* 70 and 90, however, the picture is much less clear. Some informants scored below average on the two L2 tests, as well as on the L1 reading test. These learners apparently had not developed reading skills in the L1 which could support them in their L2 reading process. Others scored below average on the two L2 tests, but above average on the Danish reading test. Their low L2 vocabulary scores may explain why these informants seemingly could not benefit from good reading strategies in their first language. Finally some informants managed to do well on the L2 and L1 reading tests but badly on the L2 vocabulary test. These learners were seemingly able to transfer good reading strategies from their first language in spite of a small L2 vocabulary. Especially two informants with fairly low scores on the L2 vocabulary test (informants no. 9 and 11, cf. Table 3) manage to do surprisingly well on the L2 reading test.

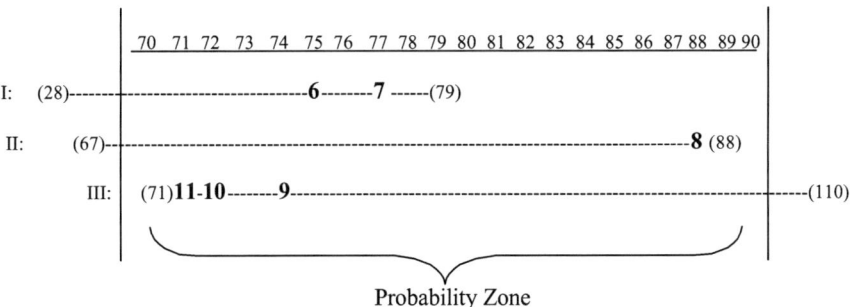

I: L2 vocabulary range for Grade 10 informants who are below average L2 readers
II: L2 vocabulary range for University informants who are below average L2 readers
III: L2 vocabulary range for Grade 10 informants who are below average L2 readers

Figure 1. Identifying a probability zone

L2 vocabulary scores below 70 seem to constitute the minimum requirement for doing well on this particular L2 reading test. Moreover all informants with vocabulary scores above 90 do well on the reading test. Thus, for the informants with L2 vocabulary scores above or below 70 and 90 vocabulary size considered in isolation seems to be a very reliable predictor of L2 reading scores. On the other hand, L2 vocabulary scores between 70 and 90 could be defined as a *probability zone* within which factors other than L2 vocabulary size assume significant roles in the prediction of L2 reading skills. The chances of performing well or badly on the L2 reading test are determined in part by L2 vocabulary size, but here we also need to pay special attention to the many other variables that influence L2 reading comprehension, e.g. L1 reading skills, lexical inferencing skills, background knowledge, or possibly a well-structured L2 lexicon. The learners who were discussed in more detail previously are indicated by their informant numbers on Figure 1 above.

Research Perspectives

In this study, a strong correlation has been found between vocabulary and reading scores in the L2, thus confirming results from previous research. Not surprisingly, the correspondence was highest for the informants with an L2 vocabulary score below 70 or above 90 on the Nation's Levels Test. As argued above, it is, however, interesting to look more carefully at the learners *within* the probability zone and discuss different factors which may influence the outcome on the L2 reading test, e.g. other factors more closely related to vocabulary knowledge, i.e. the learners' lexical inferencing skills and the organisational structure of the lexicon, aspects which have been included in our research project.

An analysis of informant 9's *inferencing success* in L2, i.e. the degree to which her guesses of unknown words in the L2 inferencing task are accurate, seems to support a relationship between lexical inferencing skills, reading skills and vocabulary size. Despite a small vocabulary, she obtained a very high score on lexical inferencing success – a result which compares favourably with the inferencing success of informants with much higher vocabulary scores. In other words, by applying adequate guessing strategies, not only was she able to outperform informants with similar vocabulary sizes on the reading test, but she also managed to surpass many of her more advanced peers. In fact, she managed to achieve the same reading score as some of the very best Grade 10 informants who boasted much larger vocabularies. A closer look at the lexical inferencing processes employed by all the informants within the probability zone may shed light on why different learners with the same vocabulary size obtain such different scores on the L2 reading test. Immediate access to lexical items is a crucial aspect of text comprehension. One could, however, hypothesise that lexical access in part is influenced by the organisation of the lexical network. An analysis of the organisation of the learners' lexicon, based on the data collected in the network sub-study of our project, may therefore add to our understanding of some of the factors that had affected the L2 reading comprehension of our informants.

Notes

[1] The authors gratefully acknowledge financial support from the Danish National Research Council for the Humanities (Statens Humanistiske Forskningsråd) in the form of a 3-year research grant, which has made this study possible.
[2] We would like to thank Dr Norbert Schmitt for his invaluable help in relation to the validation of the Danish version of the Levels Test, and Anja Knudsen for her work in the development and validation process. Any shortcomings in the development, validation and use of the test are of course entirely our responsibility.
[3] We would like to thank Elisabeth Arnbak, Carsten Elbro and the Centre for Reading Research at the University of Copenhagen for allowing us to use the Danish reading test.
[4] It is important to stress that at time 1 when the data was collected, the informants were only tested once on the L1 and L2 reading and the L1 and L2 vocabulary tests respectively. It is therefore not possible to generalise from these test results to their overall reading skills and vocabulary size in the two languages. When talking about their abilities as being above or below the average, we are thus only referring to the scores obtained by the different informants on the tests in relation to the general mean calculated for the whole informant population from both educational levels (N=60).

References

Clark, M.A. (1980) 'The "Short Circuit" Hypothesis of ESL reading – or When Language Competence Interferes with Reading Performance', *Modern Language Journal*, **64**, 203-09.

Hsueh-chao, M.H. and Nation, I.S.P. (2001) 'Unknown Vocabulary Density and Reading Comprehension', *Reading in a Foreign Language*, **13**, 1, 403-430.

Laufer, B. (1992) 'Reading in a Foreign Language: How Does L2 Lexical Knowledge Interact with the Reader's General Academic Ability?', *Journal of Research in Reading*, **15**, 95-103

Laufer, B. (1997) 'The Lexical Plight in Second Language Reading', in Coady, J. and T. Huckin (eds.), *Second Language Vocabulary Acquisition*, 20-34, Cambridge University Press: Cambridge.

Lee, J.F. (1997) 'Non-native Reading Research and Theory', in Bardovi-Harlig, K. and B. Hartford (eds.), *Beyond Methods, Components of Second Language Teacher Education*. McGraw-Hill.

Meara, P. (1996) 'The Dimensions of Lexical Competence', in Brown, G., Malmkjær,

K. and J. Williams (eds.), *Performance and Competence in Second Language Acquisition*, 35-52, Cambridge University Press: Cambridge.

Nation, P. (2001) *Learning Vocabulary in Another Language*, Cambridge University Press: Cambridge.

Qian, D. and Schedl, M. (2004) 'Evaluation of an In-Depth Vocabulary Knowledge Measure for Assessing Reading Performance', *Language Testing*, **21**, 1, 28-52.

Schmitt, N, Schmitt, D. and Clapham, C. (2001) 'Developing and Exploring the Behaviour of Two New Versions of the Vocabulary Levels Test', 55-89, *Language Testing*, **18**, **1.**

Schoonen, R., Hulstijn, J. and Bossers, B. (1998) 'Metacognitive and Language-Specific Knowledge in Native and Foreign Language Reading Comprehension: an Empirical Study among Dutch Students in Grades 6, 8 and 10', *Language Learning*, **48**, 71-106.

REVIEW ARTICLE

THE SCHOLARSHIP OF PARANATIONALISM

Ulf Hedetoft

Jørgen Sevaldsen, ed., *Britain and Denmark: Political, Economic and Cultural Relations in the 19th and 20th Centuries* (Copenhagen: Museum Tuscalanum Press, 2003), 658 pp. Dkr. 475, £43, $59. ISBN: 87-7289-750-3

As a child, I remember following avidly the vicissitudes of the Danish national soccer team pitted against better sides like Sweden, Hungary, Britain, Germany or the Soviet Union. The stakes were clear: it was less a question of Denmark winning, but rather of battling courageously and suffering an honourable defeat. Subsequently, symbolic victory to a large extent consisted in cashing in on the facile praise that the coach or players of the opposing team magnanimously bestowed on the heroic underdog. Although 'we' lost, we nevertheless won the respect of our victors in these bilateral showdowns, and by mirroring ourselves and our achievements in their recognition, we maintained and even enhanced our national self-respect.

In certain cases, one would go a step further and develop an admiration for the stronger teams and their superiority – imagined to reside in innate cultural features – which might stop just short of a secondary or vicarious form of nationalism. For many, myself included in those days, this was true of the Hungarian team of the 50s, the Brazilian of the 50s and 60s, the English of the 60s. Unlike today, the difference in the level of play between the Danish amateurs and the best national teams was so great that it was possible to nurture both kinds of national attachment at the same time. The benefits of each were very different: you could have your cake and eat it too. In this way – which for research on nationalism constitutes a well-known figure – the weak and the strong, David and Goliath, complement and mutually even constitute each other. For the weak, the selfishness (and yet insufficiency) of one's own nationalism finds an external corollary and vicarious confirmation in the attributes and performances of the Other; this often develops into a role model. For the strong (though this is less binding and therefore less frequent), satisfaction accrues from this external admiration and from the freedom of the truly sovereign to show magnanimity and to lavish praise on those trying to emulate them – as long as they do not succeed.

When later – in the mid-60s – I embarked on the study of English at the

University of Copenhagen, I found myself embroiled in a cultural environment thoroughly infused with such an atmosphere of vicarious nationalism or, as I prefer to name the phenomenon, paranationalism: a fascination, a deep-seated, seemingly irrational and totally implicit admiration of all things 'English' or 'British' (very emphatically so, rather than American, Canadian or Australian), which informed the attitude to the subject of staff as well as (most) students, and dictated a specific curriculum (the 'canon'). Approaches to texts, the world and other humans were themselves deeply inspired by Britain, British (literary) history and British institutions.

Unlike commonplace forms of national egoism, this was narcissism with a difference: the ideological-cum-cultural result of a particular *relationship* between two nation-states, one weak, the other powerful: two nations diversely conditioned in the historical cauldron of the British empire; England's language had been globally disseminated; the Danish economy depended on exports to Britain, and its statehood had been given the final twist of gratitude and intellectual support by the contribution of Britain to the liberation of Denmark in World War II. (On these topics, see in the volume under review the informative contributions to the section on 'Denmark and Britain in the International Economy and in Great Power Politics c. 1864-1914'). This deed of liberation came to constitute the ultimate stamp of approval on this asymmetric bilateral relationship and facilitated its interpretation as the 'beginnings of a beautiful friendship', a phrase used in several contributions to *Britain and Denmark* – though authors do not quite seem to agree on when the friendship actually started. Not until after 1945, as Hans Hertel suggests (p. 473), or much earlier, following the cataclysmic events of 1864 and the forced re-evaluation and re-forging of Denmark's international relations, as indicated by Carsten Due-Nielsen (pp. 171 ff.)?

On this count, I side with Hertel – and Due-Nielsen may be inclined to do the same. At least he should, since he pithily sums up the 1864-1914 period by observing that 'their [Britain and Denmark's] mutual relationship was always secondary to their relations with other countries' and that one might do well to 'concentrate on these two countries' important relations to third parties in order to explain their actions or passivity towards each other' (p. 195). There was nothing very idyllic about the *rapport* in those days: just so much hard-nosed *Realpolitik*. Denmark was caught up in a complicated game among the 'Great Powers' about the strategic importance of the Baltic Sea; it was suspended between British, German and Russian interests and foreign-policy preferences, and only by the skin of its teeth – partly due to adroit balancing, partly to sheer luck – managed to survive as an independent nation-state. The beautiful friendship – as it was widely interpreted in small-state Denmark – with its apparatus of paranational myth-making came later, after World War II, as a web of cultural constructions and ideas.

It is testimony to the strength of British paranationalism in Denmark in those days that its historical conditioning and causalities tended to be elided or neglected in favour of an almost primordialist view of the virtues of Britain and British culture. Hence, that this was a question of a historically specific *relation* – interpreted and given widespread currency by intellectuals and opinion leaders – went counter to the *Zeitgeist*. In the Department of English at the University of Copenhagen, for instance, those of us who favoured an alternative curriculum that would attend to such relational specifics were met by either indifference or open animosity. Britain was to be studied for its immanent virtues, in an atmosphere of quiet admiration, and not from an analytically dissecting and theoretically constructivist vantage point. In fact, theory was quite unwelcome. The English spirit, we were told, was empirical and empathetic – and we had better follow the lead. Theory was a 'continental' thing, foreign to the spirit and culture we were there to understand and imbibe. Given that background, it is little wonder that, as Jørgen Sevaldsen notes in his Introduction, 'Anglo-Danish relations and contacts have not been the subject of much academic interest' (p. 12). (Perish the thought that another reason might be that the relationship was always too asymmetrical to be meaningful.)

This is all, of course, entirely in keeping with the foundational principles of paranationalism. According to *Longman's Dictionary of English Language and Culture*, 'para' as a prefix has three semantic implications: 'beyond', 'very similar to' and 'connected with and helping'. For many Danes, the English nation incorporated loftier, yet comparable virtues, and for precisely this reason could be used as a booster of Danish self-confidence. The more powerful nation, cast in this role, becomes an ideal to emulate; it is to be respected by the weaker, dependent state. In retrospect, one might even obtain the satisfaction of having outsmarted the role model. In the final contribution to *Britain and Denmark*, tellingly titled 'How Denmark Made Britain Pay the Bills', this view is clandestinely embedded in Morten Rasmussen's account of the negotiations that led to EC membership for Britain and Denmark in 1973: 'the enlargement negotiations show how a smaller European country like Denmark can, inside a multilateral framework, outmanoeuvre a large European state on issues where interests diverged'. True enough, by the 1970s the beautiful friendship was fading, bilateralism was being overtaken by new, multilateral interdependencies, and uncritical admiration was slowly being supplanted by more level-headed views of the 'Atlantic Archipelago' (J.G.A. Pocock's phrase); 'Atlantic Europe', so Tom Nairn hypothesized with his 1977 coinage 'Ukania', was in decline and possibly in the process of breaking up. This leads to more directly articulated national stances in the appraisal of the David-Goliath relationship – the celebration of the strengths and virtues of smallness – even though the pendulum, in Rasmussen's case, swings too far to the other side. The Danish success in the EC application – maintaining the structure of the CAP, which was in the interest of Denmark but not of Britain – did not come about as a result of sophisticated negotiation techniques, but because the French position happened to coincide with the Danish (as Rasmussen concedes elsewhere).

So times change, as do our perceptions of them. They have, fortunately, changed so much that a major project like *Britain and Denmark* is feasible on the Danish academic scene. The relationship can, now, be addressed directly, and quite successfully too. This is much to be welcomed, though timing itself is a factor that contains its own little ironies. At a time (now) when, at least on the assumptions on which the book is predicated, bilateral relations matter little in light of globalization, European integration and multiple interdependencies, the time is finally ripe, it would seem, for a work like this. When the 'beautiful friendship' is no longer with us and (at least this kind of) paranationalism no longer plays havoc with our hearts and minds, we can be granted access to its 'real' history, habitus and implications (cultural, economic and political), protected by the distance of time and mildly saturated by nostalgia for bygone days (something which the volume does not entirely manage to steer clear of: see below). In one sense, it may in fact be said to do its best to maintain this kind of protective cushion. By choosing as its historical cut-off point the entry of Britain and Denmark into the EC, it not only preserves historical and analytical distance (fair enough, as these things go), but also studiously avoids the no less interesting contemporary impact of globality, the EU and so forth on the interactions between Britain and Denmark over the past 30 years. Here Due-Nielsen's insight, quoted above – 'their mutual relationship was always secondary to their relations with other countries' – applied as a template for understanding current relations, would have helped to put the global distortions of the bilateral illusion in a revealing perspective.

In fact, bilateralism – particularly between weak and strong states – always contains pervasive illusory features. This may be seen to detract somewhat from the many virtues of this comprehensive and informative work, one of the points where it succumbs to the deceptiveness of the 'beautiful friendship' and the lures of British paranationalism in Denmark. Where much of the empirical evidence presented demonstrates (a) that the beauty of this friendship has always – particularly post-World War II – been in the eye of the beholder, i.e. Denmark, and that in this sense it has always been a very one-sided love affair, and (b) that relations have been thoroughly shaped by extraneous factors, such as the Americanization of Europe, the Cold War confrontation, the EU and other bilateral relations (e.g. with Germany), the structure of the book, and the form in which many of the analyses are presented, draw their sap from an imagined, relatively hermetic dual relationship; and this, so we are led to believe, was not compromised until 1972 (or thereabouts).

In this vein, for instance, Hans Hertel talks about the Danish turn to 'Anglo-American cultural values from the 1920s to the 1950s' (pp. 431 ff.), by means of hyphenization thus conflating very different influences while in a different sense conceding that much significant cultural inspiration originated in the big globalizer of the latter half of the 20th century, rather than in the lesser globalizer of the first half. Britain was already then – in the 1940s and 50s – in rapid decline (a point naturally lost on British paranationals in Denmark, whose partiality was dependent on the illusion of their protagonist's power). Hertel's account (p. 440) of the influence of 'negro culture' and 'jazz culture' on Danish cultural life in the 1930s, leaves Britain entirely out of the picture – or allows for British influence 'by proxy'. Conversely, Charlotte Rørdam Larsen, in her article on 'Tommy Steele and the Notion of "Englishness"', gets the meaningful difference between English and American cultures absolutely right. 'I don't dig America', as Steele is quoted as saying (p. 502), echoing popular sentiment in Britain as well as much élite thinking in Denmark in the 1950s and 60s. A gap existed between the English-speaking cultures on either side of the Atlantic and their difference was sometimes perceived in antagonistic terms. In the Department of English at Copenhagen, the USA – and its particular versions of the English language – did not enjoy the same status and recognition as Britain. For the local anglophiles, bacon and butter, or tea and scones, had acquired a fine coating of cultural sophistication, whereas America offered nothing but gross materialism, mass culture and trigger-happy politicians. (The Danish view was of course entirely in accord with British stereotypes of America.)

It should be stated clearly that this is a worthwhile book: comprehensive, well-edited, informative and readable. As I have indicated, it fills a gap. It takes relations seriously, and it spans politics, history, economics and culture. Strangely – or maybe not – it is best and most illuminating in its treatment of events, periods and turning-points where Danish-British relations were not, or were not perceived to be, particularly close: e.g. before World War II especially with regard to political and economic interactions. Bent Raymond Jørgensen's article on 'Small State Denmark and Great Britain. The Development of Danish Trade Policy and Economic Relations with Great Britain 1929-1937' is a fascinating study. One finds, in this essay and elsewhere, illuminating exposés of reciprocal images and perceptions, whereas the section on cultural relations tends to be more anecdotal and impressionistic, and prone to the fallacies of paranational celebrations of 'the country of one's longing' (p. 488). Here too, though, we find well-researched contributions, such as Lesley Jackson's on 'Anglo-Danish Design Exchange 1900-1970'.

Nevertheless, although many of the articles in this section (and some in other sections too) demonstrate that paranational celebration of Britain is extant, and that an undercurrent of wistful and nostalgic fascination pervades the book as a whole, even the most glaring examples of this analytical modality represent an interesting twist to the old narrative: Niels Bugge Hansen's article on Brandes' contribution to the study of Shakespeare, for instance, is as much – and possibly even more – a celebration of Georg Brandes, the 'great Danish critic' (who plays an important role in the book's narrative since he 'converted' from being a Germanist to a devout Anglophile), as of William Shakespeare, the 'great English poet' (p. 404). And Inge Kabell and Hanne Lauridsen's piece on 'English at the University of Copenhagen during the 2nd World War', though thoroughly suffused with the spirit of Britishness (see e.g. p. 482), is also a direct tribute to the Danish protagonists of the English cause, Professors Jespersen and Bodelsen, and their dedication to the survival of English studies in Denmark during the German occupation.

In both cases, the fusion of England and Denmark remains the lofty ideal, but Danishness reappears as a significant co-marker of symbolic identification. Direct celebration of 'all things English' is couched in a tone of wistful regret for a lost paradise, and what has consistently been the (often intangible and invisible) point of departure – Denmark and Danishness – now reclaims its proper place. Narcissism remains, but is now – with the benefit of hindsight, the disappearance of the beautiful friendship, and the diminution of direct and major dependence on a state now regarded by few outside of Whitehall as a 'world power' – truly a narcissism of *minor* differences. Which is all very ironic of course: at a juncture when the playing field has levelled out considerably and the conditions for a proper 'friendship' – a relationship between co-equals – are at hand, this comes across as a *loss* of friendship, conveyed by a tonality of nostalgia, and underpinned by the book's wilful omission of the last 30 years. It is as though it would be too painful to trace the debunking of the historical role model. As Bo Tao Michaelis put it in his review of this volume in *Politiken* (May 17, 2003): 'all is so well and yet a bit nostalgic.... Once America seemed "farther away than Aunt Lise in the countryside", but now it is England which seems to be a rustic proposition' (my rendering). It would have been salutary to have had such changes of perspective and relationships addressed; but also to find out more about the forms in which anglophilia still survives, in spite of everything, institutionally as well as through personal contacts.

These are structurally important omissions. Other omissions are less grave but nevertheless noteworthy. One of the once important vehicles of paranational identification at the mass level – now considerably faded – is (as already recalled) English soccer; another was TV drama; a third was the youth cultures of the 1960s; a fourth, as I have been at pains to point out, was studying English at university in the 1960s and 70s; a fifth, travelling to Britain in varying personal and professional capacities, and the cultural contacts that followed. Such central issues are at best peripherally addressed. However, the most serious omission is the lack of theorization. Here the volume suggests more than it delivers. The Introduction – which frames the questions well – whets our appetite for a conceptualization of relations between small and large states (p. 11 & p. 13) as a template for understanding the Danish-British case, but small-state theory, theories of nationalism or of international politics are virtually absent – or at best constitute parts of individual contributions, but not of the overall design. Elsewhere Sevaldsen posits that 'Britain ... always provided a close and easily accessible and observable laboratory for new trends in social and political thinking' (p. 25), but this hypothesis is barely developed in the volume, with the possible exception of Carl-Axel Gemzell's paper on the 'The Welfare State: Britain and Denmark'. On this count, more rigour and a more consistent framework for understanding both processes and results would have tied together the many disparate contributions and factual-descriptive accounts; it would also have distanced the volume more convincingly from the once dominant empiricism among Danish scholars of Britain, and from the paranationalism that has for so long characterized Denmark's relations to Britain.

NOTES ON CONTRIBUTORS

Dorte Albrechtsen received her Ph.D. in foreign language acquisition in 1992 and is now an associate professor at the Department of English, the University of Copenhagen. Main research interests are processes in student writing and foreign language acquisition as well as discourse analysis of learner texts. Currently, she is involved in a large research project '*Processes in writing and vocabulary acquisition in English as a foreign language*' which has been funded by the Danish National Research Council for the Humanities

Kyoko Baba is a doctoral candidate in the second language education program at the Ontario Institute for Studies in Education at the University of Toronto. Her research interests are learning and assessment of vocabulary and academic writing in second languages.

Anna Cieślicka received her Ph.D. in linguistics in 1997. Her post-doctoral dissertation project concerns the processing of figurative language by second language learners. She teaches at the Department of Modern Languages, School of English, Adam Mickiewicz University, Poznań. Her research interests are: second language vocabulary acquisition, cognitive psychology, bilingual language processing, and figurative language.

Alister Cumming is professor and Head of the Modern Language Centre at the Ontario Institute for Studies in Education at the University of Toronto. His research and courses focus on the teaching, learning, and assessment of writing in second languages, particularly English in academic or settlement contexts.

Keanre Eouanzoui is assistant professor of Education Research Methods in the Department of Education at the Niagara University, New York State. He received his Ph.D. from the Ontario Institute of Studies in Education at the University of Toronto in 2004.

Guillaume Gentil is a post-doctoral research fellow in the Modern Language Centre, Ontario Institute for Studies in Education, University of Toronto. He will be assistant professor in the School of Linguistics and Applied Language Studies at Carleton University in July 2004. His primary research interests are biliteracy and second language writing within academic and professional settings.

Birgit Henriksen received her Ph.D. in foreign language acquisition in 1990 and is now an associate professor at the Department of English, the University of Copenhagen. Main research interests are in vocabulary acquisition and the organisation of the mental lexicon. Currently, she is involved in a large research project *'Processes in writing and vocabulary acquisition in English as a foreign language'* which has been funded by the Danish National Research Council for the Humanities.

Kirsten Haastrup was professor of foreign language education at the Danish University of Education from 1992 to 2000 and has since then been research professor at the Department of English, Copenhagen Business School. She is currently involved in a large research project *'Processes in writing and vocabulary acquisition in English as a foreign language'* which has been funded by the Danish National Research Council for the Humanities.

Paul Meara is professor of Applied Linguistics at the University of Wales, Swansea, where he runs a large distance based doctoral program. His main research interests are in formal modelling of vocabularies and simulations of vocabulary development.

Paul Nation teaches in the School of Linguistics and Applied Language Studies at Victoria University, Wellington, New Zealand. He has taught in Indonesia, Thailand, the United States, Finland, and Japan. His specialist interests are language teaching methodology and vocabulary learning. His latest book is *Learning Vocabulary in Another Language* published by Cambridge University Press (2001).

David Singleton is associate professor of Applied Linguistics at Trinity College, Dublin. His research and publications have addressed a wide range of topics, but in recent years his principal areas of interest have been cross-linguistic influence, the age factor in language acquisition and the second language lexicon.

Rob Waring is associate professor at Notre Dame Seishin University in Okayama, Japan. He has taught English as a foreign language for about 20 years in the UK, Australia, China and Japan. His main interests include vocabulary acquisition, reading development and creating a Balanced Curriculum.

Brent Wolter has held a number of teaching posts in Japanese universities, and is currently Assistant Professor of English at Okayama University. He has been a member of the Swansea vocabulary research group since 2000, and expects to finish his PhD work shortly.

Luxin Yang is a doctoral candidate in second language education at the Ontario Institute for Studies in Education at the University of Toronto. Prior to studying in Canada, she taught at the Capital Normal University in Beijing, China. Her research interests include learning and teaching English as a second and foreign language in academic settings.

Book Reviewer

Ulf Hedetoft is Professor of International Studies at Aalborg University, and Director of the Academy for Migration Studies in Denmark (AMID). His publications include *British Colonialism and Modern Identity* (1985); *Signs of Nations: Studies in the Political Semiotics of Self and Other in Contemporary European Nationalism* (1995); *Political Symbols, Symbolic Politics: European Identities in Transformation* (Aldershot: Ashgate, 1998); *The Postnational Self: Belonging and Identity* (Minneapolis: University of Minnesota Press, 2002); *Danish Immigration Research 1980-2002* (2002), and, forthcoming, *The Global Turn: National Encounters with the World* and a co-edited volume of essays on *The Politics of Multiple Belonging: Ethnicity and Nationalism in Europe and East Asia* (Ashgate).

FORTHCOMING ISSUES

- Angles on Shakespeare
  2005
  Editors: Niels Bugge Hansen and Søs Haugaard

- Studies in Translation
  2006
  Editor: Ida Klitgård

- 1707-2007: The State of the Union
  2007
  Editors: Jørgen Sevaldsen and Jens Rahbek Rasmussen